Holding On While Letting Go

Holding On While Letting Go

A Transition From Hope To Grief And Back To Hope

Learn to Dance in the rain!

By

Sharon Crislip

Sharon A Crislip

&

Surviving With Sarcasm

Getting Through Cancer Being Humorously Sarcastic

By

Jeff Merrifield

Copyright Sharon A Crislip 2015

All rights reserved. No part of this publication may be reproduced, distributed, stored in a retrieval system, or transmitted in any form or by any means, including photocopying, recording, or other electronic or mechanical methods, without the prior written permission of the author. The only exception is brief quotations in printed reviews and certain other noncommercial uses permitted by copyright law.

Contact the Author at: SharonCrislip@aol.com

A portion of the proceeds from the sale of this book will be donated to St. Jude's Children's Research Hospital in Memphis, TN in memory of my son, Jeff Merrifield

St. Jude's Children's Research Hospital was Jeff's favorite charity because they help children who have cancer and no one is turned away. The website to make donations to St. Jude's Children's Research Hospital may be made on the following website: https://www.stjude.org/

ISBN: 1514722968
ISBN 13: 9781514722961
Library of Congress Control Number: 2015910535
CreateSpace Independent Publishing Platform
North Charleston, South Carolina

This book is dedicated, first and foremost, to my son, Jeff Merrifield, and his remarkable strength, determination, and bravery in the face of his battle for life. He left fingerprints of strength on our lives.

It is also dedicated to those who are facing the same battle, those who love them, and stand by them through it all. I wish you blessings wherever your journey takes you.

My son's greatest hope was that he would leave a living legacy.

Our book is a result of that hope.

ACKNOWLEDGEMENTS

Carolyn Beever is my friend and an extremely talented artist who designed the cover for my book. Art has been an important part of Carolyn's life since the first time she picked up a brush and started her first art class at the age of six. Carolyn graduated from Mary Washington University in Virginia in 1964, and immediately began her career teaching art. She taught in elementary schools, middle schools, and high schools for forty three years. Carolyn continued her education in the field of art through the years, and obtained her Instructional Technology Certification at George Mason University in Virginia in 1995. I met Carolyn at Godwin Middle School in Dale City, Virginia, where we worked together for 20 years. She ended her teaching career at Forest Park High School in Woodbridge, Virginia, where she not only taught art, but wrote the curriculum for Computer Graphics I & II, Multimedia I & II, and Independent Studies in Multimedia for Prince William County Schools in Manassas, Virginia. Carolyn retired in 2007 and is now able to create her art work, at her leisure, in many forms of media – pen and ink, water color, oils, and digitally on the computer. Carolyn used photos, taken by me, to create the digital painting for the beautiful cover on this book. Carolyn is an amazing artist and is a member of the Fredericksburg Center for Creative Arts, where she continues to teach and create in all forms of art. Thank you **Carolyn** for all you have done to help make Jeff's dream become a reality.

Four more key people who helped me in the endeavor to keep my promise to my son **are Sherri Breazeal, Dawn Gill, Sarah Schuller, and Beth Withrow.** These four ladies worked endless hours editing, proofing, giving me feedback, answering my questions about the content of my book, and giving me encouragement. They even shed a few tears as they read about Jeff's journey through cancer, and my journey through the grief of losing my son. A huge thank you to each one of you – I would have been lost without my friends, **Sherri, Dawn, Sarah, and Beth.**

A huge thank you goes to two friends, and published authors, who influenced and advised me about the publishing of this book - **Stacy Eaton and Melvin Miles.** I can't begin to tell you how much their knowledge and expert advice meant to me. I would have been lost without the advice I received from both of them. **Melvin** is also responsible for the theme for my cover and encouraging me to use the title, Holding On While Letting Go. I truly believe God puts people in your life for a reason and I know this is true with **Stacy and Melvin.**

I would also like to thank **my family and my friends** who have been there for me every step of the way. They listened, offered suggestions, and supported me for months. Their support, words of praise, and encouragement kept me moving forward to finish this book.

A very special thank you to my **husband, Cris.** His love, support, and encouragement meant the world to me. There were times when I was so totally involved in my writing that I didn't even realize it was meal time until he would bring dinner to me. No one was more aware of my dedication to this book than **Cris.** He heard me make that promise to Jeff that I would finish his book and have it published. **Cris** knows I never break a promise, so there wasn't a doubt in his mind that I would keep that promise to my son. His support, and above all, his love helped me reach my goal.

I would like to thank all those whose help and support proved to be a milestone in the accomplishment of my end goal.

TABLE OF CONTENTS

Acknowledgements vii
Author's Note xiii

Part I	Surviving With Sarcasm - by Jeff Merrifield	1
Chapter 1	The Shortest Chapter Ever Written...Or Maybe Not	3
Chapter 2	Disclaimer...So Nobody Sues Me...Well, Go Ahead If You Want...I Have Nothing!!!!	5
Chapter 3	Pre-Diagnosis: What's Goin' On?	7
Chapter 4	Diagnosis Depression	10
Chapter 5	I'm So Confused	14
Chapter 6	Let The Games Begin	17
Chapter 7	Everybody's A Comedian	19
Chapter 8	Vanity and Cancer Don't Mix	23
Chapter 9	Hospital Attire...A Gown That Flaps In The Breeze...NOT	25
Chapter 10	That Boring IV Pole...Let's Kick It Up A Notch	27
Chapter 11	Hospital Visits...A Room With A View	30
Chapter 12	Jeff's Sense of Humor Prevailed	34
Chapter 13	Whatever...Shameless Product Endorsements	39
Part II	Holding On While Letting Go - by Sharon Crislip	43
Chapter 1	Getting to Know Jeff	45
Chapter 2	A Caregiver	48
Chapter 3	Learning from Others...Dealing with Grief	52

Chapter 4   A Mother's Promise…I Will Finish Your Book 55
Chapter 5   Poems…Finding Words of Comfort 62
Chapter 6   Life Goes On…A Year of Firsts 73
Chapter 7   Signs…Sent From Heaven 85
Chapter 8   Special Messages 97
Chapter 9   Handmade With Love…Memories Preserved 111
Chapter 10 Friends & Family - Old Memories &
            New Beginnings 118
Chapter 11 His Legacy Lives On 133
Chapter 12 His Sister Remembers 146
Chapter 13 Jeff's Story 161
Chapter 14 Moving Forward…Life Goes On 192

About the Authors 195

AUTHOR'S NOTE...

Just to make sure you know what you are about to spend your hard earned money on, I thought it only fair to explain a few things right here and now. Yes, I have been through cancer. In fact, I have had the pleasure of going through cancer not once, not twice, but three times. Yes, this is a book about my experiences and my sarcastic attitude while dealing with my most recent fights with cancer, but by no means is this some kind of autobiography. I'm sure you aren't looking for a book about coping with cancer which talks about my childhood.

Although this book may eventually be found in the "self-help" section of your local bookstore, I personally don't favor that classification. That being said, if that is where Mr. or Mrs. Book Seller decides to put this, and it gets into your hands, I am all for it. Personally, I like to refer to these pages simply as a guide that might help you release at bit of that inner sarcasm buried deep inside as you fight to become a survivor. Hence the title, "Surviving with Sarcasm". If you are looking for a guide, or "self-help" book with 30 or 40 page chapters full of medical terminology and words that use nearly every letter in the alphabet, put this book down and look at the ones on the shelf to the left or the right of mine. This one is not for you. So many books find ways to stretch chapters out by repeating the same thing over and over in different ways and end up being more confusing than helpful. Too often the initial thought a writer is attempting to convey is lost because a reader is spending half his/her time looking up terminology in a dictionary, if you actually still use a dictionary. Is it even possible to buy an actual dictionary anymore? Most likely you would be searching the internet trying to figure out what those words mean that you couldn't even spell with a can of Alphabet Soup. My point is that nobody is going to remember or even begin to grasp the idea being explained if the author rambles on and on like I have just done for the majority of this paragraph. If you are like me, you like things to get right to the point.

My idea of a guide like this one consists of short chapters that can be mentally digested quickly in the few minutes you may find in your busy day. Maybe read a bit while you are waiting for treatment or are in the middle of treatment. Also, in this hectic world, I know those free minutes in your day may involve private time in your own bathroom. Don't worry, I won't be offended. I'm not ashamed to admit that some of my best ideas come during those private times.

What I hope to convey is the attitude that helped me go from being a cancer patient to a cancer survivor. Please understand these pages will be serious and blunt sometimes, but hopefully light and humorous most times. By no means is anything meant to be offensive; however, I do tend to be very sarcastic…part of my charm, I guess. If nothing else, I hope this book guides you towards an attitude that fits your personality and helps you develop a friendship with your "inner sarcasm" that will give you strength during what may be the greatest challenge of your life.

Read on my friend and get ready to kick some cancer ass!!!

SARCASM:

Just One Of The Many Services I Offer

A Note from Jeff's Mom:
My son, Jeff, was a cancer survivor for 19 years before this demon we call cancer took his life on September 23, 2010. As you read this book, never doubt this - Jeff never gave up hope, never gave up fighting, and never gave up his humorous, sarcastic attitude until it was time for him to go home to be with God. If you are reading his book, please remember that Jeff's positivity and sarcasm, his will to fight, to live, to kick cancer's butt served him well. In addition, the awesome doctors and nurses and the availability of newest treatments because of continued research to find a cure, gave Jeff 19 years as a cancer survivor. Research continues, new treatments are being discovered every day, medical technology continues to advance. Never give up. That wonderful day is coming!

I hope Jeff's book will be a tool to give you the hope and determination to always keep fighting. I hope Jeff's book will inspire a positive, sarcastic attitude in you as you fight the fight while researchers continue to strive to find a cure and rid the world of cancer. Remember, there is always hope because YOU are alive and because YOU are a survivor. Now, take my son's advice - be positive, be determined, be sarcastic, and above all, fight to win, not only the battle you are in right now, but to be the survivor who will win the war.

Does Jeff's death to cancer make him less a survivor? No! Cancer did not win, because it was not able to change Jeff. It was not able to take away his bright, funny, sarcastic spirit. It did not diminish his love of life and people. No, cancer did not win Jeff's final battle. Jeff did indeed kick cancers butt!
~ *Sharon Crislip*

Part I

Surviving With Sarcasm

- by Jeff Merrifield

CHAPTER 1

THE SHORTEST CHAPTER EVER WRITTEN...OR MAYBE NOT

When I first started thinking about this work of art you are holding in your hands, which I am sure will soon be on the New York Times best seller list, I fully intended for the first chapter to be the shortest chapter ever written in the vast world of literary history. I really couldn't tell you whether it would have been the shortest chapter or not. To be completely honest, I didn't feel the need to research it. Call me a slacker if you will, but after the battles I have had, I'll settle for being called names.

What I thought might be the shortest chapter ever written was to be an entire two words long. "Cancer Sucks"! That was it. I guess I should tell you I fought cancer three times and I can, at times, be a bit sarcastic. I probably should figure you know that already since you bought the book, but you never know - maybe you are attracted to sarcasm or medical tragedies. Don't worry; I'm not one to judge people...too harshly. Do what you will.

While speaking with one of the many people I met who were fighting their own cancer battles, she told me that her husband got her a tote bag with "Cancer Sucks" on it. My first thought...well....I don't want to use the exact words...but anyway...time to rethink the first chapter.

Not long after that, chemo or not, I had to take my annual pilgrimage to Margaritaville with my sister to see Jimmy Buffett in concert. While walking to our seats, I saw a guy wearing a shirt that read across the front, "I Beat Cancer's Ass"!!! So the next day, I had to do some searching online and found out that there were a lot of sarcastic people out there like me. I have to admit, some of them made me look tame by the things they came up with to put on their shirts, mugs, bumper stickers, and whatnot.

Nonetheless, I found myself whipping out the credit card and buying the first of my cancer wardrobe. After purchasing shirts reading, "Caution: Chemo Crankiness", "I Have Chemo Brain, What's Your Excuse"? and "I've Had Radiation Therapy. If You Can Read This You Are Too Close", I decided an entire chapter starting a masterpiece such as this, simply stating, "Cancer Sucks" would be too ordinary. So consider yourself blessed. You have been treated to a few extra paragraphs of literary greatness.

"CANCER SUCKS"

CHAPTER 2

DISCLAIMER...SO NOBODY SUES ME...WELL, GO AHEAD IF YOU WANT...I HAVE NOTHING!!!!

I figured it would be of utmost importance at this time to include a disclaimer stating that the pearls of wisdom provided scattered, albeit, somewhat sparingly throughout these pages come from my personal experiences. At no time in my life have I been to medical school and all I know about cancer comes from my first bout with cancer in 1992, my second round in 2006, and my third time in 2010...(as if once wasn't enough). Some may think I enjoy toxic drugs being pumped through my veins, or that I like being shoved in a microwave every other decade, but honestly, I could do without it, and there are better ways to get a suntan. Oh wait... sun tanning...skin cancer...no, I am not advocating getting a suntan.

This is my personal soapbox to babble about my sarcastic attitude, how I coped with this insanity, and different things you can do to make the most of the proverbial bad situation. I know there have been studies about the importance of a positive attitude during times of crisis, but don't ask me for scientific evidence to support why I think putting a smile on your face when you feel like screaming is a good thing to do. There will be times when you don't want to smile, so don't. Find that one person who can tolerate your medically induced mood swings (Hi Mom) and allow that person to be your sounding block. However, if you have a visitor, try to force out a smile or two; it puts them at ease during a very awkward time for them.

Also, by no means is this book intended to influence anybody's decision concerning choosing their doctors, oncologists, or courses of treatments. Find a doctor you like. Well, let me change that a bit…Find a doctor with the best credentials who has nurses you like; they do all the work anyway. (Sorry docs…love you all, but it is what it is.)

Finally, allow me to apologize for the occasional harsh words you may come across here. I honestly am not trying to make this the first, for lack of better term, self-help book, with a parental advisory on the cover. It is my opinion, that if you are one of the too many to be diagnosed with cancer and old enough to read, you have earned the right to have a few blunt words cross your path. Honesty and sarcasm can be an interesting combination.

> "A smile can hide so many feelings.
> Fear, sadness, heartbreak…But it also
> shows one more thing, strength."
> ~Unknown

CHAPTER 3

PRE-DIAGNOSIS: WHAT'S GOIN' ON?

In addition to being a self-confessed sarcastic individual, in the years just prior to my latest diagnosis, I had become very vain in reference to my appearance. Five or six evenings a week, I would be at the gym working out. Having grown up the chubby kid, putting in hour after hour at the gym had me finally seeing myself in a positive light. There I was five foot seven inches, (those of you who know me personally can stop laughing…I said five foot seven inches…sure that may be with shoes, but give me that extra inch), one hundred seventy pounds, thirty two inch waist, forty four inch chest, sixteen inch biceps, and loving life. I was rockin' a short spiked up haircut. I have always joked with my family that it was a curse that I had to be the best looking person in the family, but I would carry the torch for us all. After all, somebody had to.

In the weeks before getting my life threatening and life changing Stage IV diagnosis, (the worst diagnosis you can get), I began to drop some weight. I thought the extra cardio workouts at the gym were paying off. I was actually feeling pretty damn proud of myself and thinking the whole diet and exercise thing works, but that all changed in January 2006, when I found a lump under my arm. Even though I had a previous diagnosis over a decade and a half earlier, it had been so long ago, I never thought much about it. Being one that had to feel beyond horrible before going to see a doctor, I didn't even have a primary care physician. Probably not the smartest thing considering my previous cancer experience, but I never claimed to be a genius. So, this cancer journey would start at an Urgent Care Center.

At first, it didn't seem the doctors were too concerned. Being in the middle of cold and flu season, it seemed like they were leaning towards some kind of bug or infection. As a precaution, I was sent to see a surgeon. Lacking what I thought at the time were any other serious symptoms, the surgeon wanted to wait a couple of weeks to see if the lump cleared up. Well, the lump kept getting bigger, and a few days later, I woke in the middle of the night, literally drenched in sweat. I thought maybe I had a fever that broke. After a couple more nights of waking up in a pool of my own sweat, I went back to Urgent Care. With the addition of the night sweats and more rapid weight loss, one awesome Nurse Practitioner immediately called the surgeon and insisted I not wait any longer. I was immediately scheduled to have the swollen lymph node removed and sent for biopsy.

Now it was time to wait while the reality of my situation was beginning to hit. While I may boast about my many qualities – a positive attitude, determined, being buff, handsome, humorous, and sarcastic, patient is one thing I wasn't, so waiting on the results of this biopsy was not an easy task. Little did I know, waiting would be something that would become a very big part of my life, so patience was something I would try to learn as the days passed.

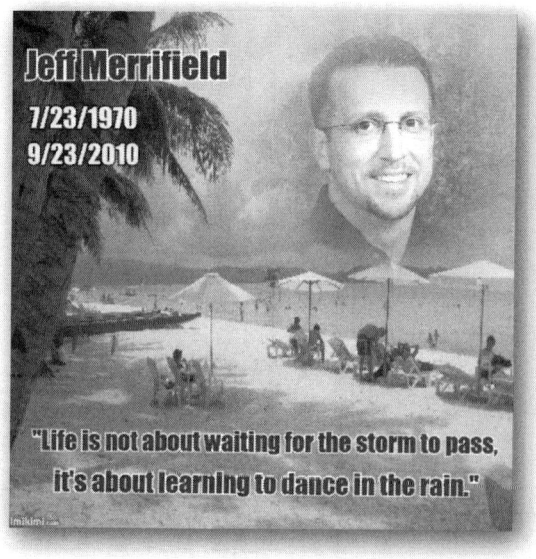

"Patience is the ability to idle your motor when you feel like stripping your gears."
~Barbara Johnson

"Once you choose hope, anything's possible."
~Christopher Reeves

CHAPTER 4

DIAGNOSIS DEPRESSION

So you have spent days and days waiting for test results, biopsy results, blood work, you name it. You have spent your days and nights trying to convince yourself there is nothing terribly wrong, but all the while feeling the time has come to say your final goodbyes. The day comes when the path your life is going to take is about to be chosen for you. One path leads to elation and relief, the other, uncertainty of what the future may or may not hold. The waiting comes to an end when you hear the word CANCER.

Your initial reaction may be shock, fear, disbelief...most likely a combination of those and a few other emotions. Your stomach turns and your eyes glaze over. Whatever the doctor is saying at this point is totally lost so don't worry about trying to remember what is being said. The exact same conversation will take place many times in the coming days. Don't even try to fool yourself at this point that it's no big deal. You are about to begin the fight of your life...fighting for your life. How depressing does that sound?

Well, go with the feeling, especially if this is the first time hearing the word CANCER in reference to your personal health. Personally, I am writing this after my second bout with the demon in 15 years. Who am I kidding? It doesn't get any easier. One question comes to mind no matter how many times you have been dealt this hand. Why Me?

So now I get to annoy the eternal optimists who will say you should never ask, "Why Me?" They will say you should be asking "Why Not Me?" Well, yes and no. Yes, there are way too many people who are faced with this type of tragedy. So the statement, "Why not you?" may very well apply when you think of all the people experiencing the same or comparable diagnosis. However, never allow yourself to feel selfish for thinking, "Why me?" If anybody ever tries to tell you differently, your diagnosis gives you the right to think whatever you want to think. There are many stages to go through when faced with a cancer diagnosis. Some will go through more than others. Even though I had been diagnosed with a different type of cancer years earlier, honestly, there is no way to avoid "Diagnosis Depression."

Feeling like you have hit rock bottom is completely normal and acceptable. People expect you to be upset and depressed, even though they are telling you that everything is going to be all right. Everybody saying everything is going to be okay, is also their way of dealing with your diagnosis. Never forget that you have so many people supporting you. These same people are also trying to find ways to cope with your diagnosis. The most important thing to remember is that no matter how horrible you are feeling, things will get better. I threw that gem in for the eternal optimists to try to keep them happy. Of course, they are always happy. They are the ones who know deep down in their happy little souls that this book will get better and be more positive. Sorry to disappoint…no refunds!!!! Wait, you can't disappoint them; they are eternal optimists. Thanks to all of them for buying my book. You made my day much better. Now don't you feel good about yourself? Just spreading my little bit of sunshine.

You may have always been one of those optimists. Way to go!!! Good for you!!! I was not one of those people. Prior to my diagnosis, I guess you could call me "cautiously optimistic." I always liked to think that whatever struggle was going on in my life, it would all work out for the better. I know I may have said the words and tried to convince myself, but it was not always easy, and I didn't always believe what I was telling myself. So even though I had gone through one cancer diagnosis years earlier, it totally sent me spiraling downwards. Even when I put a smile on my face to make everyone around me feel more at ease, I was honestly at the lowest point of my life. I knew it and couldn't fight my way out of it.

As it turned out, it was the one thing that I have avoided for my entire life that guided me towards the path I needed to be on. DRUGS!!!!!! (Legal of course, despite the temptation to self-medicate with things not necessarily medically approved.) The thought crossed my mind many times to use my Grandmother's recipe for what ails you. Whether it be a headache, toothache, or stomach bug, Gram always said, "Take a shot of whiskey", or "Try a gin-soaked raisin". Kind of makes me wonder if she really was at church all the time or a support group of another kind. (Just kidding Gram. I love you…and your gin-soaked raisins.)

When my doctors first asked if I needed anything for anxiety and depression, I said no. I had to be the tough guy. Big mistake…huge!!!! Not only was I stressing myself out, but I know now I was probably being a huge pain to my family and friends. When anxiety takes control, not only will you become horrible company for everyone that is on the journey with you, you subconsciously compensate for the chaos going on in your head by fidgeting with anything you can get your hands on. (Big shout out here to Dr. Barrett at the Medical College of Virginia at Virginia Commonwealth University for my first "Happy Pills". He noticed I was about to cut my finger off by constantly spinning my ring.)

Plain and simple…when the doctors offer you drugs…JUST SAY YES!!!! Take whatever they offer. If you have insurance, the co-pay for those wonderful little pieces of happiness is next to nothing. With all the toxic chemicals they are going to pump into your body in the coming weeks and months, never ever turn down the offer for those little "Happy Pills". Not only will they most likely be the only drugs you will be able to pronounce, but they work. Now I know why Mom kept telling me for years to go get a prescription, even before I was diagnosed. I can say now with much certainty that there may have been a few times in my life that I could have been a tad bit irritable. I feel so much better getting that out in the open. I may become an eternal optimist yet.

(Note to Optimists…Keep reading, it is going to get better…I promise.)

CHAPTER 5

I'M SO CONFUSED

It took a few days and sleepless nights, but the fog I had been in since hearing my diagnosis started to clear. The haze that had clouded my mind began to be replaced with countless questions about what my diagnosis meant. What are the "stages" my oncologists are talking about? What is "Stage 1"? What is "Stage 4"? What's the difference between CT Scans, MRIs, and PET Scans? I'm not pregnant, why am I having a Lumbar Puncture? Why do I need to have a Bone Marrow Biopsy? What do all these numbers on my blood work mean? Why do I have to go to a cardiologist before treatment? What are cancer treatment protocols? What is a chemo port?

Personally, so many questions were running through my mind I could not keep track of any of them. Just when I thought I was beginning to understand one thing, they would throw something else at me which made the stuff they told me before even more confusing. Since the extent of my medical knowledge consisted of what I learned watching medical dramas on television combined with a couple of my Grandmother's gin-soaked raisins, I had to say "SCREW IT!!!!" (Actually, I used a different word, but Mom told me I wasn't allowed to be too profane in my book).

No matter how self-sufficient I had been in my life, it was time to admit I needed help making sense of it all. I first turned to the oh-so-wonderful World Wide Web. As awesome as modern technology can be, the Internet was the absolute worst place to spend my time searching for answers to life and death issues. Talk about a depressing bunch of garbage. Do a search for your type of cancer and all you will find are countless websites of nothing but worst case scenarios. Bottom line, if it doesn't come from the American Cancer Society or another website recommended by your oncologist, it is absolutely 100% worthless.

Your time needs to be spent focusing on staying physically strong, not becoming more mentally exhausted and convinced by misinformation that there is no hope. Somebody needs to become your note taker, researcher…whatever title you want to give him or her. You need someone to go to every appointment with you and write everything down, ask all the questions and basically become your life line. Thankfully, I did not have to look far for my support system. I have a sister who is a nurse and the world's most obsessive compulsive mother who would not stop until she became a walking medical encyclopedia.

Whether it's a member of your family or close friend, allow this person to be the one who will walk with you on every step of this journey. You will be going to see one doctor after another. When you fill out all that paperwork for you appointments, make sure they are listed as individuals who have access to all your information. The last thing you need to deal with when you need something during treatment are the pencil pushers spouting laws and regulations to you about not being able to release your information to your life line. Don't get me wrong. Privacy laws are awesome and very necessary, but when you are spending twenty four hours a day coping with your diagnosis and thinking about upcoming treatments, the last thing you need to deal with is some pencil pusher behind a desk from nine to five talking to you about insurance and paperwork. All they see is paper and a medical record number, not a person. Everybody you deal with from the receptionist, to the nurses, to your oncologists are now on your payroll. Expect the best and don't settle for anything less

I'm confused, oh wait, maybe I'm not.

CHAPTER 6

LET THE GAMES BEGIN

By now, a team of oncologists are busy researching your course of treatment. If chemotherapy is involved, not only is your team trying to decide what combination of drugs to mix together, but also the best location to administer your treatment. Although my local hospital did the procedure to install my chemo port in my chest to administer drugs with names as long as my arm, and my local oncologist began a course of initial treatment, with my diagnosis being at Stage IV, and the combination of chemicals in my treatment protocol being so toxic, the hospitals and cancer centers close to home were not able to provide my treatment.

I had my treatments at Virginia Commonwealth University Medical Center of Virginia. (VCU MCV) My "chemo cocktail" consisted of several different types of chemotherapy drugs. There were times when I wondered if nurses were playing "Eenie Meenie Minee Mo", listening to what "Simon Says" or "Flipping a Coin", to see which one of those cocktail ingredients would be the first to be hung on that "Hangman" device beside my bed that they refer to as an IV pole. My oncologists were brilliant doctors, and my nurses were absolutely awesome, so in this game of "Life" we were playing, even though I was the star player, I was more than willing to take a back seat and let them decide how this game would be played.

> "You have to learn the rules of the game. And then you have to play better than anybody else."
> ~Albert Einstein

Now that the game plan has been set, the nurse decided they needed to play a game of "Darts" before my chemo cocktail was started. The "darts", disguised as needles and containing my pre-meds, were coming at me. I, for one, was relieved to know that they had played this game many times, so hitting the bull's eye was not a problem.

> "I'm too positive to be doubtful,
> too optimistic to be fearful
> and too determined to be defeated."
> ~Unknown

CHAPTER 7

EVERYBODY'S A COMEDIAN

I guess one of the benefits of being a self-proclaimed sarcastic smartass is the ability to find something humorous in the most unusual places or challenging situations. Even though I am a firm believer that no matter how horrible things may seem, and you need to have a positive attitude, I don't walk around laughing my head off. Yes, it is important to find the proverbial silver lining in every cloud. But honestly, if you are going through cancer treatments randomly laughing, I feel certain your oncologist will arrange to have your chemo administered in the psych ward instead of the cancer wing.

Being a sarcastic patient with a positive attitude is important, and might get you some extra Jell-O on the ever-so-lovely mustard yellow hospital dinner trays, but you really need to keep your eyes on your doctors, nurses, cleaning crew, maintenance staff…whoever you come in contact with in the hospital. You are going to meet many people on this journey and trust me, whether they know it or not, deep inside, everyone is a comedian.

Maybe it was because I would spend a week in the hospital getting my chemo and two weeks at home, then do the whole thing over again, but there are things I noticed during those extended visits which really got my sarcastic juices flowing along with the chemo drips. Now I never met some of the people responsible, but if by some chance they are reading this, thank you for some of my extra topics to write about.

Let's start with the people responsible for decorating and painting the whole damn place. I've heard that there are certain colors which are supposed to be calming and relaxing, but seriously folks, that is crap. I am going through chemo - calm and relaxed are being replaced with nausea and drowsiness no matter how many nausea medications they give you.

The last thing on the mind of a cancer patient is food. Why in the hell are you going to paint the walls of a hospital room pea green, corn yellow, or the color of some other vegetable? Come on folks. I saw some rooms on the cancer floor painted like a rainforest, and some with tropical fish. I realize those rooms are reserved for children fighting cancer and there is no greater evil in the world than childhood cancer, but as a diehard beach bum, give me some damn palm trees painted on the walls with rolling waves, a beach umbrella and a seagull or two. Sure would have made my hours listening to Jimmy Buffett singing about the tropics while getting my chemo treatments a lot more enjoyable. Might have even thought that was a margarita hanging from my IV pole. Probably not…but still would have been nice.

I have to tell you there is another group of individuals who work behind the scenes getting your hospital room ready for your visit. Just like in any overpriced hotel, these are the people responsible for putting together your arrival "welcome package", although never once in all my visits were there any mints on my pillow. This is a $5,000 a night luxury hotel. Think I am making that up? Wait until you get that first insurance statement. Do you think that $5000 a day covers the cost of your treatment? Oh, hell no!!! That is simply the price you are paying to have a place to lay your head and be stuck with more needles than a pin cushion. Speaking of a place to lay your head, who is the genius who decided a hospital mattress should only be two inches thick? But anyway, I digress.

Back to those folks who put together your care package before your arrival. I know they mean well, but will somebody please tell them not everybody is as sarcastic as me. Also, a reminder that they are working in the cancer treatment wing might be in order. There is nothing funnier than going in your room and finding that ever so lovely pink plastic wash basin with some necessities you may have forgotten. You will find a miniature toothbrush - one with about 6 bristles. Bet the hospital got a great deal on those. With all the money they are charging for this luxury room, how about springing for a full size toothbrush. And let us not forget the extra small tube of toothpaste that makes a travel size from your local drug store look large.

What else??? Hmm. Oh yeah. What about the extremely attractive one size fits most, paper thin, off white with blue diamonds all over, hospital gowns? The ensemble is not complete without the lovely brown slipper socks with the bumpy white treads on the bottom that are so big they fall down around your ankles. Seriously, there are a bunch of people in a sweat shop in some foreign country laughing their asses off over those. Once again, for $5,000 a day, couldn't you give folks a nice fluffy bathrobe? I will further address the garments in this wonderful ensemble in another chapter. Got you on the edge of your seat now don't I?

If that wasn't enough, I can't think of anything more important to a cancer patient than the flimsy black plastic comb and miniature bottle of shampoo. This is where the reminder to those folks comes about the cancer treatment protocols and where they are working. Somebody please tell them that chemotherapy and hair aren't the best of friends. I appreciate the gesture, but that toxic combination that is being pumped into me pretty much eliminates the need for that comb and shampoo for the time being. But once again, thank you for giving me some more material for these pages. I will try to convince myself you were trying to put a little humor into a horrible situation.

Sharon A Crislip

> "A Smile Can Hide So Many Feelings. Fear, Sadness, Heartbreak... But It Also Shows One Other Thing, Strength."
>
> ~Unknown

CHAPTER 8

VANITY AND CANCER DON'T MIX

By this point in the book, I certainly hope it is abundantly clear that a sarcastic attitude is a major part of my life. If you haven't figured that out in the preceding chapters, seriously, please, go get yourself a cup of coffee and go back to page one and start all over. Now, I'm not sure if another part of my thinking is related to my sarcasm or not, and some may say it's not a good thing, but I have to admit that in the years prior to my latest diagnosis, I had become a very vain individual. I had become addicted to going to the gym five or six days a week and took myself from being the chubby kid growing up, to feeling like I finally was happy with my appearance. It wasn't long after being diagnosed that I came to the realization that vanity and cancer don't mix.

When faced with a cancer diagnosis and preparing for treatment, I had a sense of what to expect since I went through a much milder form of cancer fourteen years earlier, if there is such a thing as a mild form of cancer. If you think about it, we all know someone who has had to fight one type of cancer or another and have heard horror stories about getting sick from the chemo or radiation. No matter how you have come to get a grasp on what to physically expect when treatment begins, there are other aspects involved that will challenge you mentally and emotionally. The trick to maintaining a positive attitude is to realize that while you may be physically sick on the inside, there is no requirement that you must look sick on the outside.

My theory is this – throw your vanity out the window and resign yourself to the fact that you will bare your butt to many, sunbeams will shine on your bald head, and those wonderful steroids will make you swell up like a balloon. So, maintaining a positive attitude, a little humorous sarcasm, a lot of determination, and dressing for success (see Chapter 9) will not only help to maintain your sanity, but will make you feel that you are ready to take on all the battles that may lie ahead.

> "It's about focusing on the fight
> and not the fright."
> ~Robin Roberts

CHAPTER 9

HOSPITAL ATTIRE...A GOWN THAT FLAPS IN THE BREEZE...NOT

If you've ever been to a hospital as a patient or as a visitor, you already know all about those stylish, off white hospital gowns with the tiny blue stars printed on them, and those wonderful brown slipper socks with the little white rubber bumps on the bottom. Damn – talk about depressing. While the doctors and nurses may think they are the best thing invented since sliced bread, I have a very different opinion.

Sure, they make it easier for your nurses to find your butt and stick you with that needle full of pain killer, but hey – I'm paying big bucks to stay in this top notch facility, and easy is a word that has been removed from my list of vocabulary words. While I am totally in favor of getting a shot to control any pain that might come my way, I don't intend to act or look like I'm sick by wearing their pukey hospital attire. (I suspect I won't need anything that reminds me of puke during my stay here.) My theory - if you look like you're sick, you will act like you're sick. If anything will make you look and act sick it is definitely wearing one of those air conditioned gowns' so No Thanks!!! Now then, if you are a person who has been diagnosed with the "Big C", and getting ready to go to battle, the one thing you don't need is to look or act sick – after all, you are on a mission to become a SURVIVOR - you need to look the part. You need to be determined; you need to stay up-beat; you need to think positively and to do that you need a wardrobe that fits your personality and your lifestyle. Now, grab your checkbook or your credit card, pull out your positive attitude and get out there and hit the mall to buy your new survivor wardrobe. You've heard the expression "clothes make the person", right? Let me tell you, if you have the "Big C" what you need is "clothes to help make a SURVIVOR!!!!" Go for it!!!

So, are you wondering exactly what a survivor wardrobe is? Let me tell you about mine. Being one who loves the beach, a Jimmy Buffet fan and a fully-fledged parrothead, my hospital gear style was totally tropical and beachy. From top to bottom – well, not exactly - my boxers were the exception. I dressed the part of a survivor. Imagine the surprised look I got when the nurse walked into my room seeing me in cargo shorts, a Parrothead muscle shirt, a baseball cap and flip flops from Margaritaville, iPod in one hand, cell phone in the other, and my computer in front of me. But the comment she made was just what I wanted to hear – "you certainly don't look like you're sick." Yes, just the words I wanted to hear. Although I really didn't think it was required, I decided to be polite and apologize for not accepting the wardrobe they provided. It made me feel great when she responded with "no problem – if you look good, you feel good – and that's what we want." Even though there will be many times when you won't feel the best, looking your best will do more for you than you can imagine. That being said, you need to have several matching outfits – which for me was shorts, shirts, baseball caps, and flip flops – at least one for each day you will be staying at this "oncology resort".

CHAPTER 10

THAT BORING IV POLE...LET'S KICK IT UP A NOTCH

While I'm on the topic of looking good, there is one piece of equipment that will become an extension of your right arm and will also require some help to look good. That piece of equipment would be your IV pole. Those things are butt ugly if you really think about it. A stainless steel, boring, gray pole with hospital gown white wheels, tubing that looks like it belongs on an aquarium, and liquid filled, clear, plastic bags hanging on a hook that looks like it should be on the end of a pirate's cane. Come on, get real – you would think someone could come up with a more modern, unique design for these things that go just about everywhere with you if you're a cancer patient. Your IV pole needs revamping, so it looks as good as you do when you're taking those laps around the floor.

I know what's going through your mind right about now – what could this guy do to disguise an IV pole and make it unique. To tell you the truth, there is really no way to disguise the pole, but you can certainly make yours unique. What made mine unique? A frog – for two reasons. The first reason – I have been a frog collector for 37 years. My frog collection started when my Mom gave me my first frog on Christmas day when I was three years old. I loved that frog – he went everywhere with me. My collection grew over the years, and frogs have always been special to me.

Little did I know how special a frog would be to me during my battle with cancer. As I'm sure you know we live in a world of acronyms. The first time I heard the acronym F.R.O.G. and what it meant, was in 2006 while I was going through my second battle with cancer. This is the second reason a frog made my IV pole different from all the others.

F - Forever R - Rely O - On G – God

Forever Rely On God - this is one of the most important things you should do while you are fighting the battle to become a cancer survivor. During one of my hospital visits a friend sent me one of the cutest, most appropriate frogs there could be to adorn my IV pole. His hands (hum – do frogs have hands?) well anyway, there was Velcro on his hands which made him very easy to attach to the pole. His very long arms (arms?) and legs that were even longer, dangled freely as his head bopped from side to side as we took our evening strolls past the nurses' station. Sometimes my frog wore a baseball cap too, but I never was successful in getting those flip flops to stay on his little feet. But, my goal was accomplished – me, dressed like I was headed to the beach (unless I was cold and had to put on my jacket) and my IV pole, adorned with my long, dangly, bright green frog brought smiles to the doctors, nurses, and patients on the Oncology floor.

These were some of the mind games I played on my journey. Most days, I played the games well, but everyone has a bad day now and then and bad days are to be expected when you're going down the road to remission. There will be days when you won't feel like getting dressed in your matching outfits, but do it anyway. There will be days when you could care less if you make someone smile, but try. There will be days when you want to stay in bed all day – do it - that's OK too. It's those days when you need to remember one thing – F.R.O.G. and Forever Rely On God – He will get you through each and every day and especially those difficult days.

Holding On While Letting Go

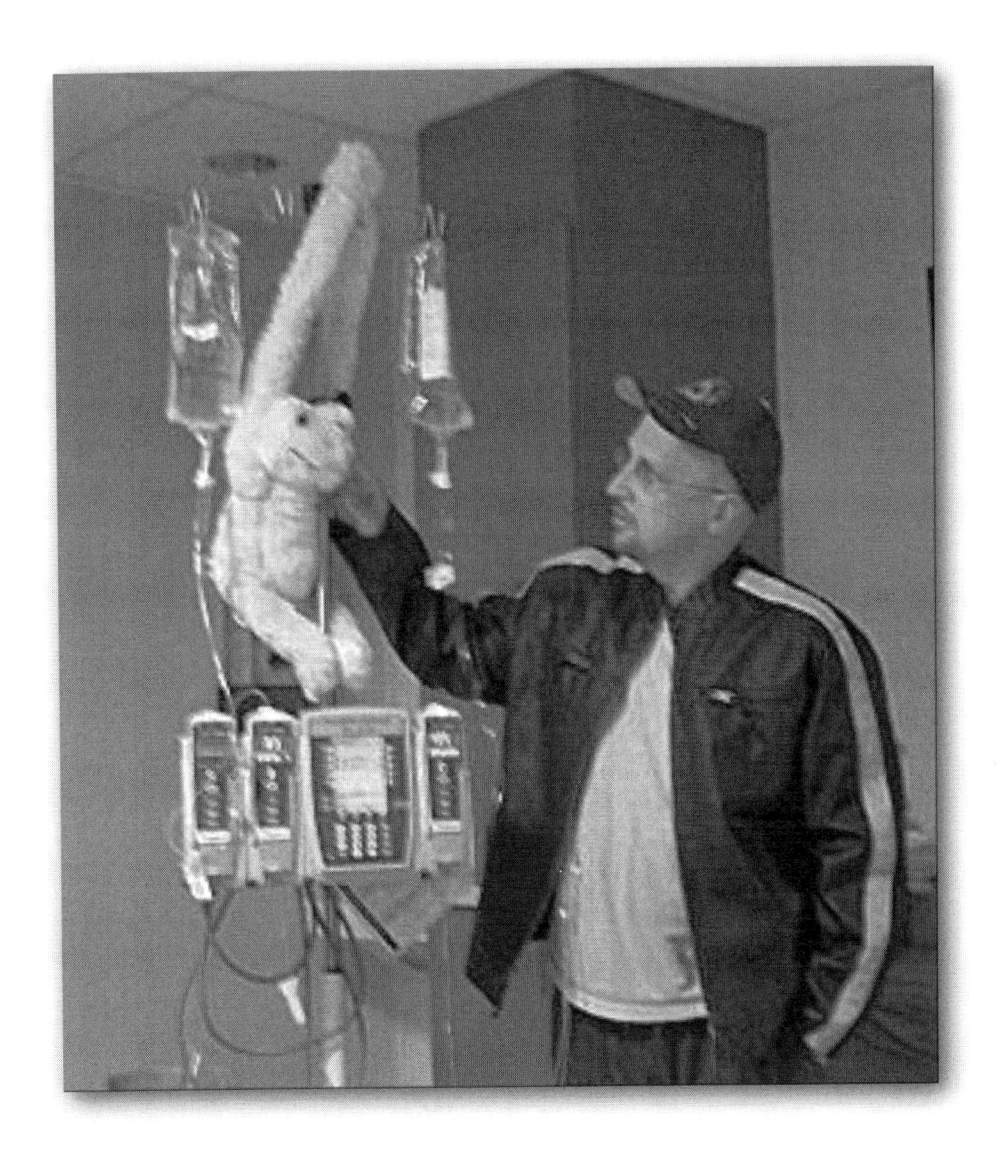

CHAPTER 11

HOSPITAL VISITS…A ROOM WITH A VIEW

My visits to the hospital for my chemotherapy treatments were many. The protocol for the chemo regime I was on meant I would be in the hospital for one week, at home for two weeks and then do it all over again. That regime led me to a month long stay in the hospital for a stem cell transplant. To me, that meant I needed a room with a view!!!

Unfortunately, many times the view was the brick wall on the adjacent wing of the hospital. There were times when my view was the top lot of the parking garage. Although that view could at times provide some interesting entertainment, it definitely wasn't the room with a view that I had hoped for. One room had a fairly decent view of the busy streets of Richmond where I could watch the cops sitting in wait of their next victim who neglected to stop for that "yellow" light. Needless to say, rooms with a great view were few and far between. The answer to this dilemma – create your own room with a view.

Once again – Mom to the rescue. She always brought something along to make our room comfortable and homey, but when I had my transplant, she pulled out all the stops. Yes, I said "our" room. Mom was beside me through every step of my journey and spent as many nights in the hospital as I did. Before I knew it, she turned my room into a tropical paradise. I think she must have bought every tropical decoration they had in stock at the local party store. Mom bought something called a scene setter to use in our room, and hung it on the wall at the foot of my bed - it was awesome. When I looked at the scene setter on the wall, directly in front of me, I was looking at a "window." As you looked "through" the window, there were ocean waves and even a seagull or two. That was only the beginning of her tropical paradise. She hung Hawaiian leis and hibiscus flowers on everything she could find to hang something on and the real hospital window was surrounded by colorful borders of tropical flowers. Bright, cheerful letters, spelled out the word Margaritaville above the window. A beachy, tropical room wouldn't be complete without a palm tree now would it? My palm tree was a small neon light on a table display in the corner of my room along with other beachy decorations. According to my mother, beach themed rooms must have a sand bucket and a shovel, so of course there was a sand bucket and a shovel in my room. Our sand bucket became the most popular item in the room. Why? It was filled with chocolate!!!

Not only did I enjoy my tropical island, so did the nurses. I am sure that I got to meet every nurse on the oncology floor - they looked forward to coming to my tropical paradise when they took their breaks. It was great – I never got lonely and they enjoyed coming to my island to get some chocolate and to spend some time with the best dressed guy on the floor!

The message I want to send you is to tell you to realize that there will be some rough days, but if you do whatever it takes to face this challenge with a positive outlook, your journey will be just a little easier. So, get your matching outfits, make your IV pole unique, and give your room a view that makes you feel good, and fight like a crazy person to reach your goal – to kick cancer's butt and become a survivor.

Sharon A Crislip

Mom's note: The sand bucket in our tropical room, which was filled with chocolate, had candy bars in it that the doctors and nurses loved. The candy had notes attached to them that were very appropriate for the hospital room of a cancer patient. Some examples of the candy and the notes were: A Tootsie Roll – **to remind you to roll with the punches.** A Snicker's Bar – **to remind you that laughter is the best medicine.** Lollipops – **To help you lick your problems.** Smarties – **to help you solve those challenging problems.** Starburst – **to give you a burst of energy.** Mounds Bar – **to give you mounds of encouragement.** Hugs & Kisses – **to remind you that someone cares about you.** Gum – **to remind you to stick with it and you can accomplish anything.** Last, but not least, is the one Jeff's caregiver's thought was great. The saying on the Take Five Bars was – **to remind you to stop in to Take Five with us when you need a break!** Seeing Jeff smile each time one of the doctors and nurses read the notes on their piece of candy made this Mom feel so good. It was fun for everyone. Jeff had intended to write a chapter titled Feed The Animals...and the Doctors and Nurses, but never got to write it. I'm sure he would have had fun writing that one.

CHAPTER 12

JEFF'S SENSE OF HUMOR PREVAILED

Jeff's Mom here – I thought this might be a good place for me to share some of the humorous moments that took place during Jeff's journey to remission. I don't think Jeff would mind me butting in to his portion of this book to share some of his humorously sarcastic moments. In addition to Jeff's oncologists and their expertise, I also credit Jeff's positive outlook on life, and his attitude through his treatments for giving him three great years in remission.

When Jeff was going through treatments in 2006, I sent out email updates to our friends and family who were praying for Jeff. In these messages, I often quoted something humorous that Jeff had said so everyone would know that Jeff was not going to let cancer take away laughter and humor from his life. I had no idea at the time that I would be finishing his book, but I'm glad that I kept copies of all the email messages and can share a bit of his humorous side with you. The following excerpts taken from some of those email messages will give you a few examples of how Jeff kept his sense of humor in one of the most difficult times in his life.

Jeff had blood work done frequently. He always went for his lab work the week before his appointments at the Massey Cancer Center Oncology Clinic in Richmond, VA. This is the conversation that took place between Jeff and one of his nurses at one of his visits to the clinic. When the nurse told Jeff about his counts, smiling he said "Ya know – I really don't like coming here thinking I feel good to have you tell me I don't." The nurses laughed and told him he might feel good, but he looked like Casper the ghost. Then he asked, "So why do I feel so good?" The Dr. told him it was because he is young and has a strong heart. The doctor also told him he was glad he felt good, but he still had to "tank" him up. Jeff just smiled and said, "I got it."

I accompanied Jeff to all of his appointments and treatments. Most times, he would get into the car, and off we would go to his appointments. We made many of these hour long trips to Richmond for appointments, so the drive became very familiar to us. One day when I picked him up at his townhouse, he got into the car saying – "Okay Mom, we're off to see the Lymphoma Wizard, but let's stop at Starbucks before you put the car on auto pilot." The Lymphoma Wizard – I couldn't help but laugh. After that, stopping at Starbucks became a habit!

One of the side effects Jeff had from one of his chemo drugs was double vision in his right eye. He wore a patch over his eye for months in hopes his vision would return to normal. One day while sitting in the waiting room at the clinic waiting on the results of his blood work, Jeff took off his eye patch to check the status of the double vision. I was reading and didn't notice him remove the patch, but I quickly looked up when I heard him say, "Oh crap." I asked him, "What happened?" He said, "I took off my eye patch to see if my double vision was improving; I looked towards the window, and I saw two baskets on the window sill." I looked over at the same window and then said - "Jeff, there are two baskets on the window sill." We both started laughing as did others around us in the waiting room. Needless to say he didn't know if there was an improvement in his vision. Jeff eventually was prescribed glasses with a prism in the lens which did correct the double vision issue. Jeff's comment to the eye doctor was "I'm a Jimmy Buffett fan and like Jimmy, I love Pirates of the Caribbean, but I am really getting tired of the pirate look at this point." Always remember, being able to find humor and laughter while going through your battle is important and really does help maintain a positive attitude.

When Jeff was told he was an excellent candidate for a stem cell transplant it was a little frightening, but also very uplifting for his mental outlook on the battle that he was facing. He was being given another chance at life. When the doctor told him about the transplant, Jeff looked down for a split second, then looked up smiling and said "If that's what we need to do, then let's do it and get it done." Jeff told me that he was a bit nervous and feeling anxious about going through the procedure; he thought he should probably feel sad, mad, or scared, but he didn't. I told him I felt certain the reason he wasn't having those feelings was because of all the prayers from his friends, family, and even people he didn't know. As we were leaving, the last comment Jeff made to his doctor was - "And to think, I was just getting used to having hair again." He followed that with, "But it's okay because I have gotten rather attached to my baseball caps."

Jeff's transplant would be done using his own stem cells. They call the procedure to gather the stem cells "harvesting". Jeff's harvesting was scheduled to be done from September 11 through September 15, 2006. Jeff, keeping his sense of humor in all of this said – "Well, at least I am staying with the theme of fall and going to be harvested…it really would have been weird to be harvested in the winter or spring." Jeff's stem cells were harvested successfully in only two visits, and he was set to begin the transplant.

In the days after the transplant, there wasn't much wit and humor taking place for a few weeks. It took all the energy Jeff had to get his strength back after the transplant. As the days went on, Jeff slowly began to feel like himself and once again his positivity and sense of humor came back.

On day 100 after Jeff's stem cell transplant, we planned a celebration dinner. Jeff wanted an Italian dinner and of course he got to choose the menu. As usual, Jeff put some thought and humor into the menu for his celebration meal and the reasons why he made those choices. "ANGEL" hair pasta because he had many angels watching over him and praying for him. Since we had so much "THROWN" at us and he had been "BOUNCED" from doctor to doctor throughout the year, he decided he wanted me to "THROW" in some "meatBALLS" too. Jeff chose a very appropriate dessert as well. Since all of our lives had been turned "UPSIDE DOWN", "pineapple UPSIDE DOWN cake" was his dessert of choice. As Jeff put it, "It's called upside down cake because all of the good stuff is on the bottom when you bake it. When you take the cake out of the pan, the good stuff that was on the bottom, has made its way to the top." Now that menu took some serious thinking.

In 2010, when the lymphoma reared its ugly head again, the trips to the doctors and hospital started all over again. One day, Jeff was being transported to the surgical floor for a biopsy, and a nurse passed by him walking in the opposite direction. Following just a few steps behind her was a custodian with a large broom sweeping the floor as he went. Jeff glanced back at the transport technician and said, "Look at that, he's trying to sweep her off her feet." The tech laughed and said that was quick thinking for someone who is on their way to have brain surgery.

As they got to the room where Jeff would be prepped for surgery, the nurse was asking Jeff all those routine questions. When the nurse said to Jeff – "Do you know what you're having done today?" Jeff's answer was, "I'm having brain surgery...I'm going to give them a piece of my mind." That comment brought laughter to the room. The nurse told Jeff that it isn't often they get someone who is joking about going in for brain surgery. Jeff told me afterwards that when he got to the operating room, he said to the surgeon "Could you please just take a little off the top?" Jeff said the doctor chuckled and was happy to see that he was able to be upbeat and positive and could keep his sense of humor during one of the most terrifying times of his life.

During his battle with cancer, Jeff's medications included steroids. Using steroids for a prolonged period of time can cause significant fluid retention and weight gain. Although Jeff wasn't happy about the weight gain, he took it in stride. Jeff's nurses knew he didn't like getting on the scale to be weighed, so they started joking with him through the weigh in process. I can't remember all the one liners they exchanged through the months, but there is one time that stands out in my mind. Jeff, with his "cocky cancer attitude" as he called it, really had fun with this one. One of his nurses told him he was so darn cute, and he was so puffy that he was beginning to look like the Pillsbury Dough Boy. When we got home that day, Jeff immediately got online and found a Pillsbury Dough Boy T-shirt with that cute little chubby dough boy smack dab in the middle of the front of the shirt. Needless to say he placed an order, and that shirt was on its way to Jeff's mailbox. Jeff couldn't wait to wear his new shirt to his next appointment. Jeff's shirt was a huge hit with the other patients in the waiting room, the doctors, and the nurses. Jeff had perfected that little "hee hee" laugh of the Pillsbury Dough Boy so each time someone poked the dough boy on his tummy, and he came out with that little "hee hee" giggle, the entire room broke into laughter. Just like the Doughboy became a global icon and had a contagious smile and cheery disposition, Jeff became a local icon at the clinic with his smile and cheery attitude wearing his Doughboy t-shirt.

Jeff's sense of humor and outlook on life never ceased to amaze me. Putting your worries and fears on the back burner and making humor and positivity part of your everyday life will help you get through almost anything.

CHAPTER 13

WHATEVER...SHAMELESS PRODUCT ENDORSEMENTS

Ok...Time to see if mentioning some of the things that became my personal "necessities" during the fight of my life will get me some free stuff. Hey, I'm not too proud to accept things. After what I have been through fighting for my mere existence...chemo, radiation, and a stem cell transplant...I think I've earned it. (Did I sound pitiful enough there? Companies don't often give free stuff, so I played the pity card. Hey... don't judge me!!!!)

#1: Jimmy Buffett/Margaritaville
Whatever trials and tribulations that you are faced with during your life, you always need to be able to get to your, for lack of better term, "happy place." "Doctor" Jimmy Buffett wrote the prescription for my own personal island paradise in my mind. From having family and friends decorate my hospital rooms with tropical décor to listening to Dr. Jimmy sing about the islands as I tried to get a few minutes of sleep before the nurses came to change my chemo bags or take my blood pressure in the middle of the night, I had to have my daily doses of Margaritaville. If anybody has ever been shoved inside a MRI tube for a scan, the drumming sound can be pretty unsettling. All I had to do was close my eyes and I was listening to island drums sitting under an umbrella on a sandy beach, feeling the ocean breeze and cracking open a cold one. Before I knew it, I would

be back in my room with a margarita hanging from my IV pole. SALT! SALT!! SALT!!!

#2: Clorox Wipes: One of the greatest products ever!
Going through an ordeal such as cancer, there are way too many lessons to be learned. It didn't take me long to realize that we live in a pretty nasty, dirty world. Take a list of items most of us come in contact with every day: a telephone, a door knob, a toilet seat, a desk. There is something seriously wrong in this world when the cleanest thing on that list is a toilet seat!!! Don't believe me? Do some research and look it up for yourself. Trust me. Have I ever lied to you? I became an expert in germ warfare when cancer came into my life. Seriously people...Clorox everything. Never give that one little mutant germ an opportunity to set you back.

#3: Cracker Barrel Country Store and Restaurant.
Sunday morning breakfast, at the Cracker Barrel became routine for me after the effects of the chemo wore off. Dressed in my survivor attire, toting the Sunday Washington Post newspaper with me, I honored the servers at the Cracker Barrel with my presence – after all, they needed this handsome face and my sense of humor to bring some enjoyment to their morning. Waiting on folks for hours can be a little monotonous, so I took it as my personal responsibility to brighten their day. It didn't take long before they began to fight over who was going to get to be my server!! No surprise there – who wouldn't want the opportunity to serve a good lookin', bald headed, cancer survivor with a great sense of humor? They kept my coffee cup filled, and made sure my Eggs In The Basket were done to perfection! An extra smile even got me a dish of fried apples for dessert!! Some may say I was playing the cancer card, but I would rather think it was my charming personality that afforded me some special attention!

#4: Purell Hand Sanitizer

Purell ranks right up there with the Clorox wipes in chemo land, especially if you've had a stem cell transplant. I consider myself a bit of an expert in germ warfare now, having had this experience more than one time. I would have a healthy bank account if I got paid for every time I took the Purell out in public to sanitize my hands. I could have made a fortune in restaurants alone since some of the best hiding places for germs are in restaurants. Menus, salt and pepper shakers, condiment bottles, buffet spoons, chairs, and more. Hundreds of people touching those items and no way to know what those people had touched and what germs they had come in contact with. Purell hand sanitizer to the rescue – comes in all sizes – keep a bottle with you at all times and put those mutant germs in their place.

#5: Reese's Peanut Butter Eggs

I became a peanut butter addict young in my life. This addiction was fueled by my mother's love of peanut butter and let's just say the apple doesn't fall far from the tree. Those little peanut butter eggs kept me sane during my fight with cancer. I believe I survived an entire month eating Reese's Peanut Butter Eggs. When I was dealing with mouth sores these eggs somehow made their way to my room. I was proud of myself for conquering the task of being able to eat an egg in just two bites. Chemo Boy was recharged and ready to fight the next round. My love of those delicious little eggs became well known to my family and friends. Before I knew it I had so many peanut butter eggs, I almost - key word here is almost - considered sharing my Reese's Peanut Butter Eggs. I didn't want to hurt the gift giver's feelings by giving away those delectable morsels that I could not resist. After all, they were gifts. A standing joke in my family was my nickname - "Chemo Boy." I remember Popeye needing his spinach to become super strong to be able to fight his villains. Along the same line, Chemo Boy needed those peanut butter eggs to be strong enough to battle that villain we call cancer.

#6: Goody Brand Combs and Hair Brushes
To my amazement each time I went to the hospital I ended up getting many "Free Products." Yep, I would get checked into my Hospital Suite on the Oncology Floor and there was always a beautiful pink container on the table. I was always thankful for that matching pink water pitcher that was included in my free hospital welcome kit. Not exactly what I had in mind when I started this chapter, but hey, at least I did manage to get some free stuff! But on a serious note here, I'm a handsome bald guy who suffers from "Chemo Brain" at times. I have to ask, why do hospitals give handsome bald chemo patients a Goody comb and hairbrush in that free welcome container? I proudly collected all those combs and brushes and thought to myself - "Regifts!!"

I'm not sure if I will ever reap any benefits from my "shameless product endorsements", but hey, it never hurts to try!

Part II

Holding On While Letting Go
- by Sharon Crislip

CHAPTER 1

GETTING TO KNOW JEFF

Holding on while letting go – that's exactly what I am doing, and I hope reading this will allow others to do the same. This book came into existence because of a promise I made to my son, Jeff, on his last day on this earth. I promised him I would finish the book he had started, have it published, and donate a portion of the proceeds to St. Jude's Children's Research Hospital. I finished his book; I have published the book; and for every book that sells, a donation will be made to St. Jude's Children's Research Hospital in memory of my son.

It is very important to me, as Jeff's mother, that you know Jeff; the real Jeff, not Jeff as a cancer victim. Jeff was an amazing person. He was a wonderful and thoughtful son, but more than that, he was my friend. Jeff and I both enjoyed being creative. We worked together making crafts' so we could take part in craft fairs – even while fighting his battle. We both loved the beach and spent hours watching the waves' crash upon the shore. We loved walking on the beach and talking as we walked. We loved life. Jeff loved helping people. Jeff was a mentor to the students he worked with as a security specialist at the middle school where he was employed. He was a trusted figure students could turn to anytime they needed help to get back on track, or someone to listen to them. Where he saw a need, he acted, and he inspired others to do the same. Jeff was a humorous, optimistic, sarcastic, determined, caring, and giving person. He was an avid Jimmy Buffett fan…Jeff was not cancer's victim.

Jeff was not only a wonderful son; he was a brother, an uncle, a grandson, a friend, and a mentor. Jeff was very special to four people all of his life, his parents and step parents – Arnold & Sharon Crislip, and Dennis & Bonny Merrifield. Family was extremely important to Jeff, and he knew he was equally important to his family as well. Jeff never fought his battle alone – he had his family beside him every step of the way as he fought so hard to live. Jeff had unending friends who were there for support as he traveled this difficult road. He always knew where he could get support, encouragement, a smile, love, and prayers. Often, there were so many people waiting to see Jeff that we had to take turns visiting, which he thought was awesome.

This is an example of Jeff's love for his family and friends, and their love for him. One of the last things Jeff did before he left us was ask me to get a note pad and pen; he wanted to make a plan for when he was well again. Jeff spoke, and I wrote - what I didn't realize at the time was that Jeff wasn't making a plan for himself. He wanted me to know the plan he had in his mind and how to carry out his wishes for his nephews. That was Jeff – always thinking of others and trying to make things better for everyone – even as his days on this earth were drawing to a close. Although he never once admitted it, I am certain he knew he didn't have much time left to spend with us.

In the end, he won the victory for which he fought so hard. In my heart and mind I know he is sitting on heavens shore watching his pug, Buddy, run along the beach. Jeff's legacy lives on as you will see when you read through the chapters of this book. As you read Jeff's story, please remember that Jeff was a son, a grandson, a brother, an uncle, a friend, and a mentor. Jeff was not a victim. Jeff was a man - a wonderful young man.

Jeff Merrifield Loving Life

CHAPTER 2

A CAREGIVER

Caregiver – a word I never really thought about, until I became one. The first time I was my son's caregiver was in 1992 when my son had cancer the first time. It was a very rare cancer, called Hemangioendothelioma. His treatments were radiation, five days a week, for three months. Jeff handled it well so I didn't really realize the true meaning of the word caregiver until Jeff was diagnosed with Stage IV Non-Hodgkin's Lymphoma in January, 2006.

By definition, a caregiver is a person who provides direct care for children, elderly people, or the chronically ill. Being a caregiver for a cancer patient means so much more to you and to the patient you're caring for. It is way more than just providing for their medical needs.

My son was diagnosed with cancer, for the second time, in January of 2006. During the first year as my son's caregiver, I discovered the true meaning of that word. I became so much more to my son than just his Mom. We became best friends; I was his advocate, and he was my lifeline. I was his researcher; he was my reason for learning everything I could about cancer. In Jeff's words, I was on a quest "to become a medical expert" and learn how to make his world a better place. I was his sounding board anytime, day or night. He was relieved to know I was always there for him. It was extremely comforting to him to know I would be there to listen and to try to help him understand what was happening. I was his note taker, the person who knew all the questions to ask; he was my reason for staying on top of everything - he made me feel needed. I needed him and he needed me – we needed each other so we could go down this road together.

We depended on each other to get through each day with prayer, love, and hope. We were determined to stay positive and focus on living life to the fullest. We quickly came to realize that every day is a gift from God, and we were determined to make each day count. I will cherish the memories of being my son's caregiver forever.

Believing in the power of prayer, I, as Jeff's caregiver, sent out daily updates via e-mail to family and friends. They in turn forwarded my messages to their friends. I can't begin to tell you how many people across the United States, and even a few foreign countries, added Jeff to their prayer lists. Jeff was added to prayer lists of churches around the world. I felt being a prayer warrior for my son was one of my most important responsibilities as his primary caregiver. Jeff told me many times that I was his guardian angel. He told me he didn't know how he would get through dealing with this demon we call cancer without the best caregiver and best Mom anyone could have. Those words are precious to me - words I will never forget - words I will treasure forever.

My son went into remission in October 2006, but even then, in my eyes, my role as caregiver did not end. My son was an adult; he had returned to his job, and was quite capable of doing everything on his own. After all we had gone through together during that year, Jeff realized my need to stay involved in his fight against cancer. Both of us were living with that "what if" fear that cancer brings to so many people. I was still his caregiver, but my role changed from primary to secondary caregiver. Even so, he knew without a doubt, that I would be there for him any time he needed me – day or night. I believe Jeff knew how much I needed to continue to be a part of his journey, so he asked me to be his back-up record keeper. I kept track of follow-up appointments, medications, tests, scans, etc. He wanted me to be involved and to be a really important person in this part of his journey.

Jeff had been in remission for three years when our worst nightmare became a reality – his cancer reared its ugly head once again. Not only did he need me as his Mom, but once again, he needed me as his primary caregiver. We went through the next nine months together, exactly the same way we had in 2006, needing each other to get through each day. Sadly, Jeff lost his battle with cancer on September 23, 2010. My heart was broken, but my son was no longer in pain, and for that, I was grateful.

When it comes to cancer, being the primary caregiver can be very frightening. The fear of not knowing what to do can be overwhelming, but trust me when I say, when someone you love needs your help, you will know what to do. Start by praying, and remembering that God will help you through every single day. A caregiver needs to listen with their heart as well as their ears. Remember, as difficult as it is for you as a caregiver, it is more difficult for the person who has been diagnosed with cancer because that person has fears beyond belief.

As a caregiver, you must remember that there will be times you feel sadness beyond comprehension, anger, overwhelmed by the enormous responsibility before you, and terrified. At these times, please be kind to yourself. You are still human with human emotions, even while you are taking on a super-human job. Allow yourself to truly feel your emotions. This doesn't mean that you aren't fulfilling the need for your loved ones; it just means that you are also acknowledging your own role as mother, son, daughter, or child…whatever the case may be. It is absolutely okay for you to show your loved one your emotions. Those cracks in our armor are what make us human, and make us love one another. Just don't allow yourself to dwell in the dark places. Feel them; walk through them, and come out on the other side!

Be proud to take on the role of a caregiver – be an advocate, a researcher, a special friend, a sounding board, a prayer warrior. Be loving, understanding, and compassionate, and treasure every minute of every day that you can help your loved one through their battle with cancer. Above all, listen not only with your ears, but with your heart, and you will be the ultimate caregiver.

> There may come a day that I
> won't be able to help you,
> But the day will never come that I won't try.
> ~L.R. Knost

CHAPTER 3

LEARNING FROM OTHERS...
DEALING WITH GRIEF

After losing my son, I felt the need to seek out other mothers who had lost a child. I needed to find out how others were able to get through the first year without a piece of their heart. I joined two online groups, Compassionate Friends and Journey of the Survivor, which were created especially for grieving mothers. I realized one thing every quickly. It didn't make a difference how old your child was, when he or she was gone, a mother's grief was the same. I found comfort in sharing my grief with these mothers whom I had never met, and I benefited from reading about the different ways other mothers were dealing with the grief of losing a child. I also realized that there were some mothers in these groups who were stuck in the grieving process for many years. I knew I didn't want to live the rest of my life in the grieving process. I knew my son wouldn't want that either. I carefully chose who I would correspond with, knowing I wanted to stay as positive as I could and learn how to be happy again. I chose those who were trying to move forward with God's help, prayers, and memories of happy times. I wanted to keep my son's memory alive not only in my own heart, but also for my family, my friends, and my son's friends.

Fortunately, I am a member of a wonderful, loving church and have a supportive church family. It was comforting to know they were there to share my pain when I needed them. The bereavement group at our church is awesome. They provided me with four booklets, one every three months, during the first year that explained the different stages of grief. I was amazed each time I received a booklet that I could totally relate to everything that was written in them. I think it was when I was reading the second booklet that I realized I wasn't alone in this process – everyone who loses a child or a family member has almost the same feelings as I was having.

Another person who was especially helpful to me was my Hospice grief counselor. It was as if she knew exactly how I felt and what I was going through. I had questions, she had answers, and she had suggestions to help me deal with the sadness and emotions I was feeling. She called me once a month during the first year after losing my son. People who work with Hospice are amazing and I am so thankful that they were there to help take care of my son. I'm so grateful that they also care enough to take care of those who are left behind.

In addition to the help and comfort I found from my family, friends, online groups, my church, and Hospice to get through my grief, I began reading books written by people who had near death experiences. Reading these books helped me in a way no one else could. In each book I read, the person gave a description of Heaven. I can honestly tell you that thinking about my son, now in such a wonderful place and home with God, eased the pain I was feeling as much, if not more, than anything else. After reading the first book, I must admit I wasn't sure I believed what I read, so I decided to find another. Again, a description of how magnificent it was in Heaven. There were things in one book that weren't in the other, but there were also many things that were almost identical. Their description of the beauty in Heaven is amazing, and I am convinced that my son is happy and healthy again, pain free, and surrounded by beauty that is like no other. At the time I started writing this chapter, my son had been gone eleven months. Although I miss him terribly, and many times my heart is filled with sadness and loneliness, I am okay because I truly believe Jeff is home, with God. I believe Jeff is always surrounded by the magnificent beauty of Heaven that I read about.

It has now been five years since I lost my son. To this day, I find comfort in the descriptions of Heaven I read in those two books. I wasn't able to obtain permission to use those descriptions in this book, but I would like to suggest that you read <u>Flight to Heaven</u> by Captain Dale Black, and <u>Heaven is For Real</u> by Todd Burpo. I also encourage you to accept the support of others through grief counseling, either online or in person. If you have the option of a Hospice counselor, don't hesitate to lean on them to help you through one of the most difficult times in your life. I relied heavily on my church family and their bereavement group for prayers and support during that first year and hope you will do the same. Life as you know it will never be the same again; but in time, you will find a new normal in your life, and you will be able to smile again.

> This is my wish for you: Comfort on difficult days, smiles when sadness intrudes, rainbows to follow the clouds, laughter to kiss your lips, sunsets to warm your heart, hugs when spirits sag, beauty for your eyes to see, friendships to brighten your being, faith so that you can believe, confidence for when you doubt, courage to know yourself, patience to accept the truth, and love to complete your life."
>
> ~ Author Unknown

CHAPTER 4

A MOTHER'S PROMISE...I WILL FINISH YOUR BOOK

I am about to embark on a journey to fulfill a promise. This was a promise I made to my son to finish his book. In January of 2006, I was not only Jeff's Mom, but also his primary caregiver. That is when he was diagnosed with Stage IV Non-Hodgkin's Lymphoma. It was a year of uncertainty, appointments, tests, scans, waiting rooms, treatments, and hospital rooms. It was a year of days upon precious days my son and I spent together. In October 2006, after having a stem cell transplant and holding our collective breaths as Jeff waged a very personal war with his cancer, we were elated to hear the doctors announce that he was in remission! Jeff remained in remission for three years. In January of 2010, my role as Jeff's caregiver was to begin again when cancer reared its vicious, ugly head once more.

In 2006, rarely a day went by that Jeff and I weren't together. We shared almost everything. I say almost because I know he purposely didn't share some of his moments of fear and sadness with me during his battle. That was my son, always trying to put others feelings in front of his own needs, especially his Mom's feelings.

Jeff and I spent weeks at a time in a hospital room at the Medical College of Virginia/ Virginia Commonwealth University (MCV/VCU) Hospital in Richmond, Virginia. That would convert to hours upon hours of what I now think of as quality time we spent together. We laughed, watched TV, listened to music, played on our computers, saw a plethora of doctors and nurses, and we waited for test results. We had what seemed to be endless conversations about anything and everything you could imagine, including this book and the many different things he would write about.

Although Jeff's writing was much more sarcastic - in a humorous way - than mine could ever be, I believe I should finish the last chapter of his part of the book before finishing Jeff's book with my thoughts and experiences as his caregiver. We often talked about the chapters he was writing for his book and what they would be about. I am certain he would want me to share a few more of his thoughts in Chapter 13, Whatever…Shameless Product Endorsements. I'm not sure I can do justice to his sarcastic side, but I promised my son that I would finish the book he was so excited about writing, so I will give it my best shot. (Jeff would have something sarcastic to say about that word "shot" but I'm new at this, so I'll not spend time on that right now.)

The author's note and the first eleven chapters you will read were written by my son. I added chapter 12, and finished chapter 13. Jeff started writing early in 2007 while he was recuperating from the stem cell transplant he had in October of 2006. When his blood counts rebounded sufficiently, and he regained enough strength, and his energy increased as well, he returned to his job with the school system, working as a security specialist in a middle school. Jeff was full of excitement and enthusiasm about getting his normal life back, but that meant his writing took a back seat for a while.

Late in 2009, Jeff decided it was time to get back to his writing and finish his book. He wrote another chapter or two before he began what would be the most difficult time of his life. In January of 2010, we learned that Jeff was no longer in remission. Once again we begin the saga of uncertainty, appointments, tests, scans, waiting rooms, treatments, and hospital rooms. To quote my son, and use the two words that he had once decided would be the shortest chapter he would write," Cancer Sucks". As in the past, Jeff's determination and positive attitude prevailed. He was ready to fight another battle with the evil demon we call cancer.

What we didn't know when the cancer came back in January of 2010, was that after a stem cell transplant, if the cancer returns, it could become more aggressive than ever before. This turned out to be true in my son's case. He had top notch doctors and nurses taking care of him, giving him the best care possible and following newly discovered treatment protocols, but the cancer cells became resistant to each drug that Jeff was given. It was extremely discouraging to take two steps forward and one step backward time after time, but Jeff never gave up trying. Jeff was amazing; he was my hero - his attitude, his determination, and his will to live and fight this battle were unending.

On July 23, 2010, Jeff celebrated his 40th birthday. He was feeling good; the side effects of the latest chemotherapy treatments had left him. Jeff was ready to party!! We had one fantastic party - the theme was from a Jimmy Buffett song – "A Pirate Looks At 40". Jeff's special day was filled with fun, tropical decor, pirate decorations, and delicious food. "Cheeseburgers in Paradise" – from another Jimmy Buffett song - were at the top of the menu. Awesome friends and wonderful family came from near and far to make Jeff's birthday a day to remember. Friends were having their pictures taken as pirates and the day was filled with laughs and great conversations. I heard more laughter on Jeff's birthday than I had heard in years. Jeff was really happy to see a very special visitor - his little black pug, Buddy. Ben Riley, Jeff's best friend who lived in Savannah, Georgia, was taking care of Buddy while Jeff was going through his treatments. Jeff was thrilled to learn that Ben had brought Buddy with him to help him celebrate his 40th birthday. Jeff's birthday was an amazing day for him and everyone who came to celebrate with him – and especially for me. To see Jeff smile, hear him laugh, and watch him enjoy being with his family, friends, and his dog was everything a mother could want for her son who had been living a nightmare. July 23, 2010 was undoubtedly the best day of that entire year for Jeff, his friends, and our family.

Jeff Merrifield
1970-2010

One week after Jeff's 40th birthday celebration, it became obvious that the chemotherapy treatments had stopped working again. What I didn't tell you previously is that when the cancer returned in January 2010, it was in his brain and central nervous system – two of the most difficult places to treat with chemotherapy. Jeff had every chemo drug that would penetrate the blood brain barrier, as well as IMRT (Intense Modulated Radiation Therapy) on the tumor that was in his brain. At this point, we knew he was in trouble, but Jeff still didn't give up – his fight continued.

Unfortunately, the enemy kept fighting too - more tumors began to invade his body. It was then that Jeff was put into Hospice care. I will never forget the first time the Hospice social worker visited Jeff. She was a wonderful, caring person who had Jeff's comfort and best interest at heart.

When she asked Jeff if he had any goals or wishes he wanted taken care of, he quickly let her know that he didn't like those words. He told her he was going to graduate from Hospice because his work wasn't finished yet.

I've always believed that God has a plan for each of us. God's plan for Jeff was that he be with Him, where he would be healthy again and pain free. I believe Jeff is with God in heaven and will forever be a happy "Pirate Looking at 40", doing the work that God wants him to do.

I have read true stories written by people who have had near death experiences and have shared their experiences by writing what they saw in heaven. After reading these accounts, I really feel Jeff is with God living an eternal life in a wonderful place. I imagine him walking down streets of gold and silver under the brightest white illumination surrounded by soft clouds in the glorious blue sky, gazing at mountains shimmering with more colors than a rainbow. I envision him seeing the vibrant shades of green in the trees and stepping on the soft, plush blades of grass, smelling the wonderful aroma of many beautiful flowers. I imagine him watching the reflections of this beauty in the ocean's water, as he goes about his timeless day doing the work that God had planned for him. My mind's eye sees Jeff in his new home - one of God's beautiful castles - where there would be many other angels with him waiting for God to give them another assignment.

I have had what I like to refer to as "signs from above" that enable me to feel that one of God's assignments for Jeff is watching over me and the rest of his family and friends. That being said, I would never want Jeff to be disappointed in me, which is why I will keep the promise I made to my son on the day he left us. I will finish his book and hope to be able to encourage countless people to be determined, to have a positive attitude, and even throw in a little sarcasm now and then as they are on their journey to become a Survivor.

Sharon A Crislip

The Cord

We are connected,
My child and I, by
An invisible cord
Not seen by the eye.

It's not like the cord
That connects us 'til birth
This cord can't been seen
By any on Earth.

This cord does its work
Right from the start.
It binds us together
Attached to my heart.

I know that it's there
Though no one can see
The invisible cord
From my child to me.

The strength of this cord
Is hard to describe.
It can't be destroyed
It can't be denied.

It's stronger than any cord
Man could create
It withstands the test
Can hold any weight.

Holding On While Letting Go

And though you are gone,
Though you're not here with me,
The cord is still there
But no one can see.

It pulls at my heart
I am bruised...I am sore,
But this cord is my lifeline
As never before.

I am thankful that God
Connects us this way
A mother and child
Death can't take it away!
~Author Unknown

CHAPTER 5

POEMS...FINDING WORDS OF COMFORT

Through the years, as a mom and as a Caregiver, I listened, I observed, and above all, I learned so many things from my son. As my son was going through his journey, fighting, as we called it "The Big C," I never thought about how unbelievably connected Jeff and I were.

There are so many things in a relationship with a son, a daughter, a spouse, or a loved one, that we take for granted. Believe me when I say, it's the little things that you miss the most like walking on the beach, roasting hot dogs over a campfire, opening gifts on Christmas morning and enjoying those special birthday dinners. Sharing new ideas about a common interest – for Jeff and me, that common interest was being creative and artistic - is something I would love to be able to do again. The one thing I miss the most are those short but sweet phone calls – "I love you Mom, just called to say goodnight" or "Hey Mom, let's meet for breakfast and solve all the world's problems."

As I listened to my son's words and observed his actions during the most difficult time in his life, I learned to always have faith that if God brings you to it, He will get you through it. I realized that I needed to keep a positive attitude regardless of the difficulties that were put in my path. I became aware of the fact that there are no guarantees in life, so I truly need to enjoy the gift of each new day. My son taught me that smiling truly is contagious and that you really can brighten someone's day with a smile. Watching Jeff go through his battle taught me not to be afraid to depend on my friends and family for all the love and support I need.

Most importantly, Jeff and I both learned the importance of the power of prayer and that we should focus on four words in the prayer that God taught us to pray - The Lord's Prayer – and those words are "Thy Will Be Done".

As the days and months went by, not only did I stay focused on the words "Thy will be done", I began to focus on the words of the poem that follows –

I just want to make you proud,
My heart screams and it screams loud,
I love you so, my son, my friend,
I always will, there is no end.
There is no end and there is no goodbye,
Now I say "we will meet again one day - up there in the sky!"
~Author Unknown

The author of this beautiful and meaningful poem is unknown, but it so perfectly describes the thoughts and feelings I had as I tried to accept that God's will had been done.

Alone

You left me here all alone,
To carry on with you gone.
It's hard to go on every day,
Since you had to go away.

I miss your help and the way you were there,
No matter what, you would always care.
You were my strength and you made me believe,
I could do anything, but now I grieve.

I can't call you on the phone,
I can't go see you at your home.

Sharon A Crislip

The pain hurts so much inside,
Some days I think I can't survive.

Why did you leave me? Why did you go?
I need you still, didn't you know?
I miss you so words can't say,
So much emptiness is in me today.

I held your hand and I stayed near,
I tried to be strong, but shed a tear.
Oh what I wouldn't give to see,
A smile on your face, now pain free

Although you're gone, you're with me still,
Your memories no one can kill.
You fought so hard, like no one could,
You suffered in pain, more than one should.

And on that day you went to rest,
I was told "God takes the best".
But I did not want to believe,
You were gone and had to leave.

And so I sit here and I cry,
Wishing never to say good-bye.
Where are you now? Are you near?
I want to know, are you here?

I just want to make you proud.
My heart screams and it screams loud,
I love you so, my son, my friend,
I always will, there is no end!

~Author Unknown

The last stanza of this poem says it all, especially the last two lines. I love you so, my son, my friend. I always will, there is no end!

Realizing how meaningful words can be when put into a poem, my daughter Kim (Jeff's sister) and I decided to put some of our thoughts and feelings into a poem. I would now like to share with you some of the words we wrote.

Ode To My Brother

I ache, I grieve, I cry.
Those looking at me from the outside
Say it will get easier as time goes by.

Although it's been days since God took you to His Heaven in the sky
I ache, I grieve, I cry, and I ask the question why?

Not an hour goes by without me thinking or speaking your name,
I know from this experience my life will never be the same.

Though there were good times as well as bad
I only seem to remember the fun that we had.

It's hard not to question why God took you so young,
There was so much left to do, your life had just begun.

I look up at the moon, the stars, and the Heavens wondering if you're looking down on me.
But I know that when the daylight comes you will send rays of sunshine falling upon me.
Although we were Parrotheads one hundred percent of the way,
"Seasons of the Sun" is the new - old song I sing every day.

Sharon A Crislip

We were full of joy and we did have fun in those seasons in the sun,
Those hills that we climbed may have been just seasons out of time.
But we had fun in those seasons of the sun,
And those stars that we reached were indeed just starfish on our beach.

September 23rd, 2010 marked my forty-third year on this earth.
Now we will share this day together as the day of your new birth.

Although I ache, I grieve, I cry, and ask the question why,
I'm very proud to share this day with my brother in the sky.

All our lives we had fun and we did have seasons in the sun
And those hills that we climbed were our seasons out of time.
~Kimberly Merrifield Crislip-Hatcher

My Only Son

My only son has passed away,
But I will love him until my dying day.
So listen to my memories, they are all I have left
Thank you all for letting me talk about Jeff.

I see his smile and those eyes so brown.
Jeff was never one to let you down.
He was strong, he was brave; he challenged his pain
With his life we had everything to gain.

We learned from his faith even in death
He brought us closer to God with every breath.
My precious son, I loved you like no other
I thank God every day for choosing me to be his Mother.

~Sharon Crislip

Sharon A Crislip

Come With Me

The Lord saw you getting tired
and a cure was not to be,
So He put his arms around you
and whispered, "Come with me."

With tearful eyes, we watched you suffer
and saw you fade away,
Although we loved you dearly
we could not make you stay.

A golden heart stopped beating
a beautiful smile at rest,
God broke our hearts to prove
He only takes the best.

It's lonesome here without you
we miss you so each day,
Our lives aren't the same
since you went away.

When days are sad and lonely
and everything goes wrong,
We seem to hear you whisper,
"Cheer up and carry on."

Each time we see your picture
you seem to smile and say,
"Don't cry, I'm in God's keeping
we'll meet again someday."

~Rhonda Braswell

A Brighter Tomorrow

Help my sorrow to release,
So I may find inner peace,
Take away my cries and tears,
Remove from me all doubts and fears.

I want to walk in the light,
To make it through this dark night,
To find happiness in being alive,
Even though my son has died.

Does this pain ever go away?
Will it gradually ease each day?
There's not a moment you are separate from me,
Together always, in memory.

In this way there is no death,
Because you live in every breath,
A physical change, but not of the soul,
The spirit remains vibrant and whole.

With Heaven's aid and direction,
I still feel our love and connection,
Supporting me in this terrible sorrow,
With the faith to believe in a brighter tomorrow.

      Copyright © 2010 C.A. Stevenson
      http://AMothersTears.blogspot.com

Little Did We Know

Little did we know that morning that God would call your name.
In life we loved you dearly, in death we do the same.

It broke our hearts to lose you, you did not go alone.
For part of us went with you the day God called you home.

You left us peaceful memories, your love is still our guide.
And though we cannot see you, you are always on our side.

Our family chain is broken and nothing seems the same.
But as God calls us one by one, the chain will link again.
~Author Unknown

We Thought of You with Love Today

We thought of you with love today
but that is nothing new,
We thought about you yesterday
and the day before that too.
We think of you in silence
we often say your name,
But all we have is memories
and your picture in a frame.
Your memory is our keepsake
with which we'll never part,
God has you in his keeping
we have you in our heart.

We shed tears for what might have been
a million times we've cried.
If love alone could have saved you
you never would have died.
In life we loved you dearly
in death we love you still,
In our heart you hold a place
no one could ever fill.
It broke our heart to lose you

but you didn't go alone,
for part of us went with you
the day God took you home.

He saw that you were getting tired
and a cure was not to be.
So He put his arms around you
and whispered, "Come with Me."
With tearful eyes we watched you suffer
and saw you fade away,
Although we loved you dearly
we could not make you stay.
Your heart full of love stopped beating
your strong, beautiful hands at rest,
God broke our hearts to prove to us
that he only takes the best.

~Author Unknown

One Day At a Time

I cannot change my yesterdays
The things that I have done.
For those days are behind me
A new day has begun.

I cannot live tomorrow
A captive of my fears.
I will face those future challenges
When that day is here.

So I have made the choice today
To be the best that I can be.
I will ask the Lord to guide my steps
And give me victory.

And I know that He will answer
True content next I find.
As He gives me strength and courage
To live One Day At a Time.
~ Judith Bulouck Morse

Never Borrow Sorrow
Deal only with the present,
Never step into tomorrow,
For God asks us just to trust Him,
And to never borrow sorrow.

For the future is not ours to know,
And it may never be,
So let us give and give our best,
And give it lavishly.

For to meet tomorrow's troubles,
Before they are even ours,
Is to anticipate the Savior,
And doubt His all-wise powers.

So let us be content,
To solve our problems one by one,
Asking nothing of tomorrow,
Except Thy Will Be Done.
~Helen Steiner Rice

CHAPTER 6

LIFE GOES ON...A YEAR OF FIRSTS

I am writing this chapter in the order that the "firsts" came into my life. My son got his "wings" in September, so I knew I had holidays approaching that would be difficult to get through. I knew it would be difficult, but I was determined to try to be a rock for my family. I prayed for the strength to get through one day at a time. In my heart, I had a feeling Jeff would be with me every step of the way. Today, I believe I was right – Jeff was with me during that first year, and I believe he always will be.

It was extremely difficult to face each day after losing my son, but I knew, somehow – some way, it was something that I had to do. Although my memories of those first few days are still somewhat clouded, I will never forget the beautiful memorial service we had for Jeff. Our pastor prepared and gave the perfect eulogy to honor my son. Jeff's family and friends spoke from their hearts about their memories of Jeff. The Elvis Presley version of "I Did It My Way" was playing in the background, a song that fit Jeff perfectly. The church was filled with family, friends, and co-workers who filled my heart with joy. The sadness was overwhelming at times, but the outpouring of love for my son was totally amazing. I got through the first of many firsts I would face during the year that followed.

Our family always celebrated birthdays and holidays together, so I knew those days would be the most difficult days to get through. Knowing Jeff would want his family to move forward and try to be as happy as we could be without him with us, we tried to make each event special, but different from what we had done in previous years. Two of my grandsons had birthdays within the first three months after Jeff left us. I knew it would be a challenge to get through them and make the boys birthdays happy for them. We kept them low key, and made Jeff a part of each birthday. We had dinner together, talked about Jeff and what he would have done if he were with us, we had our birthday cake and ice cream, and did the best we could without him with us. No one felt like singing, so we decided we would skip that part of the usual celebration. We all decided what we did worked so it was a unanimous family decision that we would do the same for all birthdays that first year. We all felt that talking about Jeff while we had dinner kept him a part of the birthday celebrations.

Next, Thanksgiving was approaching. I couldn't help but ask myself – how will I ever get through Thanksgiving dinner without Jeff sitting at the table with us? My mother and brother came from Pennsylvania to spend Thanksgiving weekend with us. Having Jeff's grandmother and uncle there made our family holiday at least bearable. My "Beach Mom", Mary Parr, gave me and idea to keep Jeff with us at our Thanksgiving dinner that I really liked – sharing special memories of Jeff. As I was getting our Thanksgiving feast on the table, I asked that everyone share a special memory of Jeff as Mary suggested. It was wonderful – we didn't talk about how much we missed him not being there; we were all very much aware of how much we missed him. We talked about how much it meant to have had Jeff with us for Thanksgiving dinner during all the years he was with us. We shared memories of Jeff that were special to each one of us. Jeff was always the one to make jokes and keep us laughing when our family got together, so it wasn't hard to come up with a happy memory. We gave thanks that God allowed us to have forty years with Jeff and that Jeff left us with many wonderful, happy memories. I asked the blessing before our meal which was extremely difficult. When my emotions started to take over, I quickly ended the prayer, and we picked right back up with good memories of past Thanksgiving dinners. Memories are precious; try to make your memories part of every day, especially holidays. Your memories will keep your loved one in your heart and part of each and every day.

Mary also suggested that from this point forward, we replace the words "I miss" with "I remember". Changing two simple little words can make a huge difference, they did for us.

> "Grief is like the ocean; it comes in waves, ebbing and flowing. Sometimes the water is calm, and sometimes it is overwhelming. All we can do is learn to swim."
> ~Vicki Harrison

I was feeling more in control as the Christmas holidays approached. I felt I had gained strength through prayer. I also gained strength from online grief groups by reading how others got through their first Christmas. I gained strength from my Hospice grief counselor and the grief group at my church. I thought I was prepared for my first Christmas Eve service at church without my son. It didn't take me long to realize that was not the case. It was too soon after losing my son to even begin to think I was ready to face such an important, spiritual holiday without him. Gaining strength and feeling like you're in control is good; being strong and being in control so soon after your loss is another story.

Every Christmas Eve, for many years, our entire family attended church together. My husband sat on my left, my son on my right, and my daughter and her family to the right of my son. For years, my son held my hand as we held our candles high and sang Silent Night. I wanted to be strong for my son and for my family for this first Christmas Eve service, but I immediately realized it was way too soon. Getting through an event that had been so special to our family, without my son holding my hand, was something I wasn't at all prepared for. Tears? Yes, lots of tears. Knowing there was no way I could get through the candle lighting and singing Silent Night, we decided to leave the church that Christmas Eve as that part of the service was about to begin. Leaving early was a good decision; I wasn't ready, and although I didn't realize it at the time, it was OK that I wasn't.

Will I ever be ready to attend the Christmas Eve service and sing Silent Night in the candlelight, I'm not sure.

Christmas Day was equally as hard, but together, we made it work. Christmas was Jeff's favorite holiday which made it even more difficult to get through. Each year, our family gathered at our home bright and early on Christmas morning to see what Santa had put under our tree. Jeff was always our "Santa" and handed out all the gifts. I knew, without a doubt, we had to do something totally different on our first Christmas without Jeff. My oldest grandson, Trey, decided he would have everyone come to his home on Christmas morning. After we had breakfast together as a family, Trey took over for his uncle and gave everyone their gifts. Unlike years past, Christmas day was quiet and sad - but together, we met yet another challenge without Jeff with us. There is just no easy way to get through the year of firsts without feeling sad and missing the one who is no longer with you. What is important is that you try, and you do the best you can, one holiday at a time. To me, the words of this poem says it all.

Missing You at Christmas

Every day without you,
since you had to go,
Is like summer without sunshine,
and winter without snow.

I wish that I could talk to you,
there's so much I would say,
Life has changed so very much,
since you went away.

I miss the bond between us,
and I miss your kind support,
You're in my mind and in my heart,
and every Christmas thought.

Holding On While Letting Go

> I'll always feel you close to me,
> and though you're far from sight,
> I'll search for you among the stars,
> that shine on Christmas night.
> ~Author Unknown

The holidays are over but winter is still with us. Jeff loved winter and snow, and he was my own personal meteorologist. My heart was sad when the first flakes started to fall, and there was no phone call from Jeff to let me know it was snowing. I missed him calling to remind me to be careful if I was out and about. I missed his calls as we waited on the "schools will be closed tomorrow" announcement to be made. Trey and Matt, my two oldest grandsons, took over the snowflake alerts which have become quite special to me. I will forever think of Jeff when the snowflakes begin to fall. I will forever miss those phone calls from my son. Now, having my grandsons fill that role, I will look forward to calls from them on those snowy days, keeping the tradition going that was started by their uncle Jeff.

Knowing that Valentine's Day without a card and a special note from my son would bring on a few tears, I decided I would try to be one step ahead. Being a sentimental person, I keep every card my children give me, so for the first Valentine's Day; I decided I would look through those cards from years gone by. Yes it was sad, yes I shed some tears, but I also read the notes in those cards and smiled when I looked at my son's handwriting. It worked for me; it was extremely comforting and made me feel closer to my son. I will continue to read Jeff's cards and notes for many years to come.

Something totally unexpected happened that first Valentine's Day. Later in this book, you will read that Jeff wanted his Dad and me to travel and asked that we start with going to Disney World – one of his favorite places. That is where we were for my first Valentine's Day without our son. It was a happy, magical place, but I couldn't help the sense of sadness I was feeling. My husband and I sat down, and I looked up to the sky as I often do. I couldn't believe my eyes when I saw a perfect heart shaped cloud in the sky at the Magic Kingdom, over Cinderella's Castle. I had been taking pictures before we sat down, so my camera was ready to capture this wonderful sign from Jeff. I did get a Valentine from my son after all.

Easter was one holiday that our family wasn't always together. This made it easier for us to get through this holiday. Spring break from school was the week before Easter. My son and I worked for a school system and my grandchildren attended school. Folks who work at a school or attend school are always excited about spring break. Often, we ended up going in many different directions for spring break. This meant that we weren't always together on Easter Sunday. What I did miss was that phone call from my son wishing me a Happy Easter. There is always something you will miss when it comes to spending a holiday without that special person who is no longer with you. Once again, reflect on all the special memories of years gone by.

Holding On While Letting Go

Mother's Day was by far one of the most difficult days to get through. My daughter, my husband, and my grandchildren were wonderful, attentive, caring, and loving. Still, my son was gone, and there was a huge void that couldn't be filled. It was Mother's Day, and it was the first time I really stopped to think that I would never again spend another Mother's Day with both of my children. With the love and support of my family that surrounded me, and my memories of past Mothers' Days, and a wonderful sign from my son, I made it through another first. A song I heard just days after losing my son was titled "If I Die Young" by The Band Perry. After hearing that song, I couldn't wait to see a rainbow. In the chorus of the song, they ask the Lord to make the loved one who died a rainbow so he could shine down on his mother so she would know he is safe with God when she stands under the colors. Those words in that song stayed with me as I continued to wait for my rainbow. I couldn't believe my sign from my son on Mother's Day was a rainbow, and yes, it did shine down on his mother. I knew Jeff was safe as I stood under those beautiful colors.

Father's Day was much the same; but again, with memories, love and support, from our family we got through yet another difficult day.

The next event our family faced was Jeff's birthday. It was an extremely difficult day for me and for our entire family. For the longest time, I had no idea what we would do to make Jeff's birthday a special day. Many say butterflies are a sign from your loved one, and I am no exception. Every time I see a butterfly, I smile and say, "Hi, Jeff." What better way to remember Jeff's birthday than with butterflies? We planted butterfly bushes in our yard in preparation for the butterfly release we would have on Jeff's birthday. I prepared a birthday dinner and Jeff's favorite cake - chocolate with peanut butter icing. We invited family and friends to come and help us make this day special. While we had dinner together, special memories of happy times with Jeff were shared before we adjourned to the outside for the release. Many tears were shed as I held the little white box of butterflies in my hand while my husband read the poem, "The Broken Chain". When he finished the poem, I released twelve beautiful Monarch butterflies, one by one. It was amazing to see them spread their wings and fly after they had spent so many hours asleep in their beautiful little white box. They flew in different directions upon their release, but thankfully, a few of them decided to stay right there with us. They fluttered past us onto the trees and bushes as if they knew we needed them to stay where we could see them. We watched them fluttering from the bushes to the trees for quite some time before we decided it was time to have Jeff's birthday cake. Family, friends and precious little butterflies helped us through another difficult day. I'm not sure what we will do in years to come, but I do know that I will always do something to make Jeff's birthday a very special day in our lives.

Holding On While Letting Go

Last, but not least for me, was getting through our summer vacation at the beach. From childhood to adulthood, our family enjoyed beach vacations together. My son was an avid beach fan. I truly believe it was the highlight of his life. My husband and I and took our first trip to the beach one week after losing our son. We walked on the shore, hand in hand, talking through our tears. We talked about all the wonderful years we had at the beach with our children and grandchildren. We stopped, and I looked up at the sky. It was then that I saw a heart and the letter "J" above it in the clouds. It was then that I realized Jeff was watching over us. It was then that I realized Jeff was telling us that life goes on, and he wanted us to be happy again. It was then I vowed that I would do everything I could to keep Jeff's memory alive. The ways that I make sure Jeff's legacy lives on will be shared in another chapter.

Dove Release

Our first year without Jeff was difficult, but we remembered him in many ways. We wanted to celebrate his Angelversary in a very special way. We were at our home on Hatteras Island, NC when a friend suggested a dove release. Elizabeth Browning Fox (Liz) and her Hatteras Doves helped make Jeff's Angelversary very special. Releasing doves is an amazing way to honor the life of your loved one. We met Liz and her doves at her home along the Pamlico Sound, in Frisco, NC, where she told us about her special doves and instructed us on how to release them so the birds wouldn't be frightened or hurt. Standing there holding those beautiful white doves, lifting them towards the sky over the beautiful water in the Pamlico Sound, and watching them fly off towards Heaven to deliver our messages that we whispered into their little ears, was a breathtaking experience. I will forever be grateful to Liz and her Doves for giving us the opportunity to release them to deliver our messages to Jeff. We all know that those doves don't really make it all the way to

Heaven, but at that moment in time, when we released each little dove with a message of love from our hearts, they were indeed taking our messages to Heaven to our son. Holding those sweet, soft doves in our hands was a wonderful feeling of peace and seeing them fly towards Heaven was amazing.

The year of firsts is not an easy one. We move on to the year of seconds, thirds, fourths, and so on. None of them will ever be the same, and none of them will ever be easy. In time our wonderful memories of all the years gone by will replace the extreme sadness of the year of firsts. In time, we will learn that our "missing" person was indeed a blessing in our lives. In time we will realize our memories will get us through these difficult days. How much sadder would it be if we had to live without our memories? I hold my memories of time spent with my son closely to my heart. On hard days, I reach into my mind and my heart to pull out those memories to help me get through. I do not dwell on my loss; I revel in the love that we shared and the time we had together. Trust me when I tell you that talking about your loved one and relying on all the wonderful memories of your time together will help you get through the most difficult days.

Yes, the year of firsts was, often times, inconceivably difficult, but I made it through, and believe, me…you will too. Though it may seem like your life is fractured, you will put the pieces back together. The end result will never be the same, but you too, will find your way to a new normal and a different kind of happiness.

"Trust in the Lord with all your heart; and don't lean on your own understanding. In all things acknowledge Him, and He shall direct your way."
[Proverbs 3:5, 6]

CHAPTER 7

SIGNS...SENT FROM HEAVEN

> When angels visit us, we do not hear the rustle of wings, nor feel the feathery touch of the breast of a dove; but we know their presence by the love they create in our hearts.
>
> ~Unknown

My "Eye" Sea Shell

The moment I found this sea shell, I knew it was special. I have always been a firm believer that, if you are open to them, you will find signs from above to let you know your loved one is okay. It was on Sunday, October 3rd, the fourth anniversary of Jeff's stem cell transplant, and exactly one week after his funeral, that I feel I received my first sign from Heaven. My husband, Cris, and I were at our home at the beach in North Carolina – one of Jeff's favorite places.

We decided to take a ride on the beach and look for sea shells and pieces of driftwood – something that we did with Jeff when he spent time at the beach with us. There had been a storm the day before, so there should have been a plethora of shells and driftwood to be found. We drove along the ocean, watching the waves break and listening to the relaxing sound of those waves as they were crashing on the shore. It seemed strange to us that the day after a storm the beach was clean – no shells and no driftwood. We thought maybe we would have better luck if we walked.

We parked the SUV and walked for hours as we talked about Jeff and remembered all the fun times we all had on the beach. Again, we found nothing – the beach was bare - not one shell and not one piece of driftwood, so we decided to call it a day and go home.

As we were driving up the beach to the exit ramp, I saw sand dunes just like I had seen many times before. I have hundreds of pictures of the beach, the ocean, and sand dunes and never once did I ask my husband to stop the SUV so I could take a picture of one specific sand dune. But for some reason, this particular sand dune looked amazingly beautiful with the sunlight shining on the sea oats, so I just had to stop to take pictures.

This dune was at least seventy yards from the ocean, but as I approached the dune, I noticed what I thought could be a sea shell buried in the sand. The shell was about two feet above the base of the dune. One lonely sea shell, upside down, and almost totally covered with sand. A day later, I remember thinking that I described finding this shell with words that pretty much described me. A lonely Mom with my world turned upside down, feeling like my world had been buried in the sand. I bent down to pick up the shell, fully expecting it to be broken. I turned the shell over and was shocked to find, not only a perfect shell, but the only shell in sight. I'm not sure of the proper name of these shells, but we call them "Eyes." Of course, me being me, and always wanting to find a sign, I thought to myself – I'm sure this means that Jeff is keeping an "eye" on me. I put this perfect shell in my pocket, snapped several pictures of the dune, got back in the SUV, and Cris and I continued on our way back to the beach house.

I was thrilled with my perfect shell, my sign from Heaven, and happy to be able to think that Jeff was keeping his eye on me. As I was cleaning the shell, I noticed there were scratches on it. I remember being a little upset that it wasn't a perfect shell after all because of the scratches. But then, it almost took my breath away when I realized that one of the scratches was the letter "J". The letter "J", the first letter of my son's name – a coincidence? I think not. As I inspected my special shell, I looked closely and realized there are two J's on the shell - a small one underneath the big one. They are going in different directions, but there was no doubt that two of the scratches were in the shape of the letter "J". My heart skipped a beat as I ran to show Cris what I had discovered. We just looked at each other and smiled. Then we realized that if you turn the shell and look at the two "J's" in a different way, it looks like J C - Jesus Christ perhaps?

When I showed my special shell to my family and friends, they too studied it and found even more meaningful symbols in the scratches. Beneath the "J's", my cousin Karen found a small cross; to the side of the cross is yet another "J". The symbol that totally convinced me that I was sent a sign from Heaven was found by my cousin Lori. I handed the shell to Lori and asked her if she could see the "J's" and the cross. She looked at me, looked back at the shell, and said "I don't see those yet, but I do see a cancer support ribbon." My special shell had never left my sight, why I didn't find the ribbon is beyond me, but it is there. Who would have ever imagined that a sea shell, scratched as it was being tossed in the ocean waves, would have so many meaningful symbols on it and would become a treasure to a mother in search of signs to let her know her son is safe with God in Heaven?

Losing a child or a loved one can make you feel like that sea shell as you are being tossed around in the ocean of life. Many events, just like those scratches on my sea shell, have left meaningful memories to help me through my loss.

There isn't a doubt in my mind that this shell is definitely a sign from Heaven and was sent especially for me.

My Heart In The Clouds

Even as a child, I had a fascination with cloud formations in the sky. I am from that generation of kids who spent time lying in the grass looking at the sky to see what we could find in the clouds. Back then, I didn't have anything special that I was looking for. Having years of experience, it was easy for me to find signs in the clouds.

During that same week, after we lost Jeff, my husband I were still at our beach house. We had many happy times there with Jeff and that's where we wanted to be to reflect on memories of the past. One afternoon as we were walking along the ocean, remembering days gone by, I looked up at the clouds and there in front of me, I saw an opening in the middle of those puffy white clouds. I couldn't believe my eyes when I saw that opening was in the shape of a heart. This was the second time in one week that I saw a heart in the clouds. To some, it may not have been a perfect heart shape, but to me, it was perfect. To me, it wasn't just any heart, it was Jeff, sending his Mom love from above, straight from his heart.

My "Son" Flower

It was the last week in October – a month after losing our son - when Cris and I arrived home after our beach trip that we noticed something growing in our yard, beside the wagon wheel at the end of our driveway. It was a strong, sturdy type plant, about twelve inches high, which at the time we thought was probably a weed. But, it just didn't look like a weed; it had a pod on the top. We decided to leave it to grow and see what it would become.

Within a few days, the plant more than doubled in size and the pod was beginning to open. We were both amazed when that pod opened into a big, beautiful, bright yellow sunflower. So, here we are. It was the last week in October and there had already been a frost in Fredericksburg, Virginia. Our yard is totally mulch with trees, mums, and hostas planted in it – no other flowers. Our neighbors don't have flowers in their yards and there was not another sunflower anywhere in our neighborhood. Keeping in mind that this was the end of October and sunflowers bloom in July, we knew exactly how that sunflower made its way to our yard. We had another frost the first week in November and yet this flower stood tall and bright.

This sunflower, standing tall and firm against the odds, of course, brought to mind the unfailing strength and faith that Jeff had shown. Because of this I have chosen to call this strong, healthy, sturdy plant a "SON Flower." I know in my heart Jeff is somehow responsible for this beautiful "Son Flower" that grew in our yard months after its normal growing season. I saved that "Son Flower" pod so I could plant the seeds the following year. I planted those seeds, but not one flower grew. To me, this was further proof that Jeff was indeed responsible for my "Son Flower" that appeared in our yard a month after he became and Angel.

I searched the Internet to find the meaning of a sunflower. "No flower can lift spirits quite like sunflowers can. Bright and cheery, bold yet comfortable, the sunflower evokes feelings of warmth and happiness. Additionally, the sunflower is often associated with adoration."

The sunflower ("Son Flower") in our yard, that appeared out of nowhere, and grew at the end of October and into November – yes, I am certain this was another sign from Heaven.

My White Feather

The afternoon of October 30, 2010, I had some shopping that needed to be done. It was my oldest grandson's birthday - Trey was turning 19. Trey had been extremely close to his Uncle Jeff, so I knew it would be a very difficult day for him. This day would be the "first of many firsts" that our family would go through without Jeff. Our family always came together to share birthday dinners, and of course, the birthday cake. I wasn't sure exactly how we would get through my grandson's birthday celebration so soon after losing my son. Knowing we had to try, there were preparations to be made, which meant I had to go shopping. Driving to the store with tears in my eyes, I tried to think about what Jeff would want us to do. I knew the answer – he would want us to make Trey's birthday a special day. As I went through the automatic door at Target (one of Jeff's favorite stores by the way), looking down as I wiped my tears away, I saw the ultimate sign lying on the floor - a white feather! As I picked up the little feather, I couldn't help but look up, smile, and say, "Thank you, Jeff."

Finding a white feather after the loss of a loved one is the ultimate angelic sign. I had been looking for a white feather for weeks. I especially looked at the beach where one would expect to find a feather, but none were to be found, until I went to Target. Now why would there be a white feather in the doorway inside Target? Why was it I found my white feather on this particular day? I am certain I know the answers to those questions.

The results of another Internet search will explain why I will always treasure my little white feather from above. "Feathers are a common form of communication from your angels and are the ultimate angelic sign. If you have prayed to the angels for guidance or for a sign that everything's going to be okay, be sure to notice feathers, especially white ones." Rarely will you find one left by an angel without knowing what it means. They can appear as tangible objects on the ground or floating from the air. You may even notice a random image of a feather, such as on television or on the side of a moving truck.

Angels use various means to get your attention and let you know they are here to help.

A Dream? Or a Visit?

It was January 2011, not long after our first Christmas without our son. I had been crying while I was thinking about my son. I remember feeling exhausted and laying down on the sofa in our family room to try and take a nap. I woke up, anxious to share with my husband the wonderful dream I had about Jeff.

In my dream, Jeff sat down beside me on the sofa. He was healthy and smiling and I remember he was wearing a green shirt. I remember Jeff leaning over me, his hand on my arm, saying, "I'm okay Mom" with a big smile on his face. Next, in my dream, I walked into my study. The door in my study opens to a flight of steps that goes down to our garage. When I walked into my study, the door was open. As I was standing there wondering why the door would be open, Jeff leaned back into the open doorway, now wearing a light purple shirt and sunglasses, again smiling and healthy. Smiling at me, he said, "It's Okay Mom" and then he was gone. When I awakened, I felt a sense of warmth and peace. I immediately went to my husband and told him I thought we should call our travel agent to plan our first trip to Disney World.

Jeff loved Disney World and asked that we go there for him when we started traveling in our motor home. The dream was so unbelievably real. I felt certain that Jeff had been right there with me. I saw him looking happy and healthy; I saw him smiling at me, and I heard his voice telling me he was okay. I somehow knew that Jeff was letting us know he wanted us to be okay too. Before Jeff left us, he made us promise to travel, and I was sure he was letting us know he wanted us to make that promise become a reality. Until the day I had that dream – or visit as some have told me – I couldn't even begin to think about traveling and having fun. That dream was the first turning point in our journey though the grief of losing a child. I don't dream about Jeff often, and I've never had another dream that was anything like that special dream on that day in January. That dream, I do feel, was a visit from our son and one I will never forget.

My curiosity about why Jeff had on two different colored shirts and why I specifically remembered those colors led me to do a little research on dream interpretation. I doubt there is any scientific knowledge behind these meanings, but guess what – the meanings I found seemed to fit my situation at the time. Since my theory on getting through grief is to do whatever it is that works for you, that's what I did. I felt there was a reason I noticed and remembered the colors of the shirts Jeff was wearing in my dream. When I read the meanings that follow, I found out why.

If You Remember a Color, It's Probably Important: If you remember that something is a certain color, it's probably important. After all, we don't really go through our day to day lives and identify the color of every object we come into contact with. So if you dream of an object that is a certain color, don't dismiss it - that color very might well be tied to the greater message of the dream.

Green: Green is another cool color that can signify peace and tranquility. Green is a color of healing and hope. Green can often mean "go". The appearance of the color may also be a way of telling you to "go ahead". Green can symbolize newness and freshness. It can also symbolize money, wealth, riches, and prosperity.

Purple: Purple, the combination of blue and red, is considered to be a very spiritual and majestic color. It is sometimes associated with royalty and good judgement. Purple is a very creative and inspiring color and possesses a mixture of compassion with calmness.

from: mindfuldreamer.com

My "J" Cloud

It was February 17, 2011 and I was driving home late in the afternoon. It was one week before we were scheduled to start our cross country trip – a trip Cris and I promised Jeff we would take when the time was right. This trip would begin at Disney World, as Jeff requested. That day, because it was a busy time of day for traveling, I had decided I would travel home on the back roads – country roads instead of the highway. To get to the back roads, I had to pass Beville Middle School – the school where Jeff had worked for 17 years. Of course I started thinking about Jeff as I passed by the school where he spent so many years of his life.

As I was driving and thinking random thoughts of happy times Jeff and I spent together were going through my mind, I glanced up at the sky and saw this weird little blob of white against the darker sunset. That blob of a cloud was the strangest looking little thing. Imagine my surprise to see this blob turn into a cloud in the shape of the letter "J" as I was watching it. I didn't believe what I saw. All I could think of was taking a picture because no one would ever believe me!

Now, I know that it is very dangerous to send text messages while you're driving, but never have I heard anyone say anything about taking pictures. Although I knew it wasn't the best idea, I had to try to take a picture.

Knowing the sun was about to set was the main factor in deciding to take the back roads home. I had been thinking I might see a beautiful sunset along the way; I had taken my camera out of the case and laid it on the seat beside me. Today was the first time I have ever done that and what do I see but a sign from my son? I was very glad I had my camera beside me when that strange little blob of white turned into a perfect cloud in the shape of a "J". A coincidence? I don't think so.

The photo is a bit blurred, and I had to darken the picture slightly so the "J" would stand out. It's a little hard to find, but if you look to the right of the house roof, and just above the tree line, you will see it. The only white in the sky and it was in the shape of a "J". I know, without a doubt, that "J" in the sky was a sign from my Jeff.

There are a few more signs that have been sent to me – pennies from heaven, four leaf clovers, and frogs, but this is already the longest chapter in the book so I'll save those for later.

I hope, after reading this chapter, that you will open your mind, your heart, and your eyes, and look for signs from Heaven. When those signs appear to you, you will get a wonderful, peaceful feeling inside. You will smile - perhaps with tears in your eyes - and you will know that your loved one is showing you that everything is okay.

> You don't get over it, you just get through it.
> You don't get by it, because
> you can't get around it.
> It doesn't 'get better, it just gets different.
> Everyday...Grief puts on a new face....
> ~ Wendy Feireisen

CHAPTER 8

SPECIAL MESSAGES

Butterflies

April 13th, 2011 was a beautiful, cool, crisp morning at the KOA Campground in Statesville, North Carolina. My husband, Cris, and I were on our journey home from our first RV trip after losing Jeff. It was a trip that fulfilled a promise that we made to Jeff to travel and enjoy life. We had done our best to embrace the experiences as Jeff would have wanted, but the loss was still fresh and raw. In some ways, I was glad it was winding down, and we were headed home; in others I dreaded going home to face my new reality of Jeff not being a daily presence in my life.

Before getting on the road, Cris set up the grill on the picnic table on our deck to cook bacon and eggs. I was standing on the deck, looking out over the lake, thinking about Jeff and the events of the past year. Just then, Cris finished the bacon and went inside to get the eggs - at the same time - telling me to look at the butterfly sitting on the step of the RV. I turned around to see a gorgeous yellow and black butterfly looking back at me. Smiling, all the sad thoughts of the past year disappeared, and the heaviness lifted from my heart. That little butterfly somehow had the power to remind me that Jeff is still here with me in spirit.

Off that little fella went, effortlessly gliding through the trees, over the water, and back again. I had my camera in my pocket, so as you can imagine, after we finished breakfast, poor Cris not only did the cooking, but was now left to do the dishes and get the RV ready to roll. Where am I? I'm standing beside the lake just waiting for that little butterfly to come back – and he did. He landed on the ground just inches from my feet. If anyone had walked by and heard me talking to that little butterfly, they may have called for the men in the little white coats to take me away. As my pretty little butterfly and I were in the midst of our conversation, along came another one – imagine that – someone came looking for him and, of course, I knew just who it was. Two beautiful butterflies sitting on the ground in front of me – now I could talk to Jeff and my Dad.

Since Jeff had gone to live with my Dad in Heaven, I have always imagined them being together. It made sense to me that if two butterflies were at my feet, it was a sign that my Dad and Jeff were both right there with me on this bright, sunny morning. One thing for certain, when someone you love is no longer here on this earth with you, it helps to believe, to have faith, and be able to create your own meanings when you see one of God's tiny little creatures come to you. When you are thinking of the person, or persons, who have gone before you to be with our Father in Heaven, just believe! Believe that they are with you, never far from your side.

For the next 20 minutes, while Cris was busy inside the RV, I was outside with the butterflies just snapping pictures one after another. One minute they were on the ground at my feet, and the next they were freely soaring through the trees and over the lake without a care in the world. The next time those two guys landed on the ground in front of me, they were joined by yet another butterfly. Being an artistic and extremely creative person, and having a vivid imagination, I knew without a doubt that my Uncle Pete had joined our party. You see, I've known for years that my Dad and my Uncle Pete were hanging out up there in Heaven being mischievous just like they were when they were alive. I had told myself for months now that they were training Jeff and that before long, the three of them would be hangin' out together and having fun. Yep – it happened – three butterflies representing three wonderful people in my life were sent to me that morning. Those three little guys flittered and fluttered around me making me smile as they seemed to chase one another through the trees, never leaving the space where I was standing.

My three little butterflies were soon joined by two more of their friends. All the same colors, which of course to me means they all came from the same place and now they were all here with me - together again. Now you know, without a doubt, I have put my own meaning to those last two little creatures that joined us. You see in 2010, God had chosen three special people who were part of my life to increase his Angel population - Jeff Merrifield, Matt Carlson, and Karen Poindexter. There are many members of my family and many friends whom I have loved and were special to me who have also left this earth. Of course I think of them and have fond memories of them too, but on this day my thoughts were with those five people.

To end the tale of my beautiful butterflies, my theory is this. On that day, as I sat sadly overlooking the lake, God sent five beautiful butterflies that enabled me to smile, to use my imagination to fill my heart with joy and bring back memories of these special people in my life: my Dad, Tony Marconi; my son, Jeff Merrifield; my uncle, Pete Lucas; and two friends, Karen Poindexter, and Matt Carlson.

What is that I hear – someone calling my name? Oh – its Cris bringing me back to reality – it's almost time to check out of the KOA Campground. All the little butterflies flew away – well, all except one, and he just sat there at my feet as the others kept fluttering by, coaxing him to come with them. He wasn't ready to leave me just yet, but the time had come to say goodbye. I reached down to touch him, and he spread his little wings and flew off to join the others. I smiled as I watched them fly away - over the water and into the trees leaving me standing by the water where I had been standing when that first little fella landed on the steps of our RV.

There was one difference - the sadness I felt was gone and the sad memories had left me and were replaced with happy ones. Because of those five little butterflies, I was smiling as I hopped into the RV to continue our homeward journey.

Rainbows

By now, you won't be surprised to be reading a story about "my rainbow" – another one of what I call my signs. This magnificent, breathtaking, awe-inspiring rainbow was sent to me 7 months and 2 days after God called Jeff home. Interesting: Seven months – Jeff was born in July, the 7th month. Seven months and two days: – 7 + 2 = 9 – Jeff left us in September, the 9th month. You see, I've been waiting on this rainbow and I knew one day, when the time was right, I would see one. I imagine you are wondering why I was waiting on a rainbow – and if you're not, I'm going to tell you anyway!! No surprise there, right?

Holding On While Letting Go

You've probably figured out by now that since Jeff died, I've become a person to "stop, look, and listen" for "signs" sent to me from Heaven. I've found pennies from Heaven, a seashell with "J's", a cross, and a cancer support ribbon on it, a heart (Jeff's heart) in the clouds, and a white feather – the ultimate sign from an Angel. I have had so many signs from my son including a rock in the shape of a "J", a cloud formed in the shape of a J, four leaf clovers, butterflies, and frequently sightings of frogs pop up in stores, magazines, and other strange places; and now my rainbow. Are you thinking why frogs? Are you wondering what on earth could a frog signify to her? Remember, Jeff collected frogs, and through the months, frogs became significant during Jeff's battle with cancer! These are just some of the ways that God has soothed this grieving mother's heart.

As I mentioned previously, the week after Jeff went to be with God, I heard a song on the radio sung by "The Band Perry" titled "If I Die Young." Of course I cried like a baby back then, but the words were perfect for what I was feeling at that time. I absolutely love this song and played it often as I continued to look for my rainbow. Finally, after months of looking, hoping, and waiting, I was sent a rainbow. To make it perfect, I saw my rainbow on Hatteras Island, while standing on the deck at our beach house. Jeff absolutely loved Hatteras Island – we often called our beach house our little piece of heaven. Seeing my first rainbow over the ocean on Hatteras Island, to me, was a very special rainbow and a very special sign from my son. In the lyrics of the song "If I Die Young", they refer to the rainbow shining down on a mother, so she will know she is safe while standing under the colors. I'm sure this is the reason I love seeing rainbows.

Waiting for months to see my first rainbow, you can imagine my surprise to see another one not long after the first. It was almost eight months after Jeff went to his forever home that I saw my second rainbow. It was gorgeous; it brought tears to my eyes, and it made me smile – it was

Mother's Day, 2011 when I saw my second rainbow – a very special gift from my son.

Now that I've seen my first rainbow over the ocean on Hatteras Island, and my second rainbow in Pennsylvania while visiting my mother, I will listen to that song and smile and remember. I'll remember sitting at the picnic table on our deck when I spotted my rainbow. My husband, Cris, and I were having dinner with Dewey and Mary Parr - two special people in our lives and in Jeff's life. I'll remember telling Dewey and Mary about what we did on the first part of our cross country trip that Cris and I took in our RV – the trip that we promised Jeff we would take. I'll remember talking to them about the summers Jeff and I spent together at the beach house crafting together. I'll remember the mornings that Jeff and I sat on the deck talking, sipping our coffee, and looking out at the ocean watching for dolphins to jump. I'll remember sitting on the deck with Jeff in the evening and waiting for the beacon from the Cape Hatteras Lighthouse to shine. I'll remember being on the beach with Jeff, chatting as we looked for sea shells and driftwood and walking in the sand along the ocean. I'll remember how special it was that my rainbow appeared over that same ocean. I'll always remember seeing my second rainbow in my hometown, Lock Haven, Pennsylvania. I'll remember that I saw this rainbow on my first Mother's Day without my son. I'll remember this rainbow as a special gift from above.

I'll remember that God sent me a very special message in a rainbow because he knew how very much I needed it. Even though, at times, I wanted to question why…why, Lord, why? Even in my darkest days, my turmoil, grief, and fear…and the questions…I never turned my back on my one true source of strength. And God, in his infinite love, sent me the message that I so desired. I will remember that the Lord made Jeff a rainbow, to shine down on his mother to let her know Jeff is safe with God while she stood under those beautiful colors.

Yes, I'll remember………

Rainbow at the beach

Pennies From Heaven

Several years ago, a friend shared a story with me about finding pennies. I thought the story was wonderful and have shared it with many friends over the years. At the time, I didn't realize how much this story and finding a penny would come to mean to me. I hope after you read the story that follows, finding a penny on the ground will have a special meaning to you too.

Several years ago, a friend of mine and her husband were invited to spend the weekend at the husband's employer's home. My friend, Arlene, was nervous about the weekend. The boss was wealthy, with a fine home on the waterway and cars costing more than her house. The first day and evening went well, and Arlene was delighted to have this rare glimpse into how the wealthy live. The husband's employer was quite generous as a host and took them to the finest restaurants. Arlene knew she would never have the opportunity to indulge in this kind of extravagance again and was enjoying herself immensely. The three of them were about to enter an exclusive restaurant that evening. The boss was walking ahead of Arlene and her husband when he stopped suddenly, looking down on the pavement for a long, silent moment. Arlene wondered if she was supposed to pass him. There was nothing on the ground except a single tarnished penny and a few cigarette butts that someone had dropped. Still silent, the man reached down and picked up the penny. He held it up and smiled, then put it into his pocket as if he had found a great treasure. How absurd! What need did this wealthy man have for a single penny?

Why would he even take the time to stop and pick it up? Throughout dinner, the entire scene nagged at her. Finally, she could stand it no longer. She casually mentioned that her daughter once had a coin collection and asked if the penny he had found had been of some value. A smile crept across the man's face as he reached into his pocket for the penny and held it out for her to see. She had seen many pennies before! What was the point of this? "Look at it," he said. "Read what it says." She read the words, "United States of America" "No, not that; read further," he said.

"One cent?" "No, keep reading," he replied. "In God We Trust?" "Yes!" he exclaimed with excitement. "And?" she questioned. And if I trust and believe in God, the name of God is holy, even on a coin. Whenever I find a coin I see that inscription. It is written on every single United States coin, but we never seem to notice it!

God drops a message right in front of me, telling me to trust in Him. Who am I to pass it by? When I see a coin, I pray, I stop to see if my trust IS in God at that moment. I pick the coin up as a response to God that I do trust in Him. For a short time, at least, I cherish it as if it were gold. I think it is God's way of starting a conversation with me. Lucky for me, God is patient and pennies are plentiful!"

A few days later, Arlene was out shopping and found a penny on the sidewalk. She stopped and picked it up, and realized that she had been worrying and fretting in her mind about things she could not change. She read the words, "In God We Trust," and had to laugh and said - "Yes, God, I get the message!" ~ Author Unknown

In God We Trust is on all coins. What better way for our Angels to remind us to trust in God that everything will be okay than to drop a penny from Heaven for us to find. The story that follows is my theory on the coins my Angels send to me.

After I read the story you just read for the first time, I liked to believe that the pennies from heaven that I found were from my Dad. He went to be with God many years ago, so I loved thinking he was sending me messages by dropping pennies from Heaven. I truly believe that this message from God is His assurance that our loved ones remain with us in the love we keep for them and that it is His promise that we will be with them again in God's time. During my son's battle with cancer, it seemed I found a penny when I needed it most. I felt sure my Dad was letting me know he was with me during such a difficult time. I knew I wasn't alone.

After Jeff went home to God, I felt confused the first time I found a penny on the ground. I picked up that penny and asked myself this question. How do I know who sent me this penny? Is this a message from my Dad or is it from Jeff? Holding that penny in my hand, I looked to the sky and said – "Okay God, I'm trusting that you will let me know which one of my Angels is sending me a message." As I started to walk, lying on the ground in front of me was a dime. I picked up the dime and decided that the dime, being a larger denomination must be from my Dad. After all, my Dad had been in heaven for over 20 years, he must be my Angel who was now dropping the dimes from heaven. Jeff had only been there for a little over a week, so in my mind, Jeff was my Angel dropping pennies. Both of them were sending me a message that they are always with me! I told God I was trusting Him to let me know who was sending me pennies. After finding the dime, I created a reason that worked for me. Trusting in God, I now believe Jeff is my Angel who is dropping pennies from Heaven in my path.

For the next three months, every time I would find a penny, I would also find a dime. I promise you, this is the truth. As unbelievable as it sounds, from September 23 until Christmas, every time I found a penny on the ground in front of me, close by I would find a dime. This gave me such a feeling of peace. In my mind, God was telling me that Jeff had found his grandfather, and they were both watching over me and sending me their love.

I remember the first time I found a penny without finding a dime. At first I felt disappointed, but that quickly changed. I remembered what I said that first day I found a penny and a dime. I told God I was trusting in Him to somehow find a way to let me know which one of my Angels was sending me a message. Yes, I was the one who decided that it was my Dad who dropped the dime, but sometimes I wonder – was it me who decided, or did God put that thought in my mind? Either way, when I find a coin on the ground, I pick it up, look at it, and read the words, "In God We Trust". I know it is my faith and trust in God that has enabled me to find comfort in finding these coins that, in my mind, mean that Dad and Jeff are always with me in spirit.

It seems that I now find an inordinate number of pennies and/or dimes and they always seem to appear when I need them most. There have been days when I have felt especially sad or lonely. Those are the days I have found as many as five coins throughout the day. Is it a coincidence that each penny or dime I find on those days when I feel sad makes me smile? Is it a coincidence that with each penny or dime I find, I smile and a little bit of the sadness disappears? I don't think so. As the years go by, I realized I am finding more pennies than dimes. It is my belief that God knew I needed my Dad more than ever when I lost my son. I think God's way of fulfilling that need was to give me that dime and penny together. I still find Angel dimes from my Dad, but I think my Dad knows I've found a new normal in my life and just drops those dimes when I need them most.

I continue to find Angel pennies from Jeff on a regular basis. When I see a penny on the ground, it reminds me to always trust in God. I believe God is reminding me that an Angel is watching over me when I find a penny that has dropped to the ground. It seems I always find a penny when I need that little extra bit of encouragement. There have been times over the past few months when I wished I could find a penny and magically one appeared. Magically? Probably not. God knows when I need my Angels to be with me. God knows that I find comfort in finding a penny or a dime and thinking my Angel is there to guide me and to help me work things out.

As I finish this chapter, I will tell you an interesting tidbit about my Angel pennies. My husband and I promised Jeff that one day we would travel. Jeff wanted us to go to the place he loved and found magical. We kept that promise. The first trip we took after losing Jeff was to one of our son's favorite places - Disney World in Florida. Disney World is sparkling clean all the time. There is rarely anything lying on the ground. The maintenance crews are walking through the parks sweeping the grounds every hour of every day. As we entered the Magic Kingdom, I said to my husband, "How are we ever going to find a penny on the ground here? As soon as something drops to the ground, it is swept away." Would you believe that we found one penny at each of the parks we visited at Disney World? Each penny we found was either as we entered or as we were leaving each park. In this magical, spotlessly clean place that Jeff loved to visit, we found Angel pennies dropped from Heaven for us to find. Yes, I smiled each time I found a penny and said, "Hi Jeff." I also looked to Heaven and said, "In God We Trust."

> "So don't pass that penny when
> you're feeling blue.
> It may be a penny from Heaven, that
> an Angel has tossed to you."
> ~Charles Marshbum

Occasionally I find a nickel or a quarter and wonder "who" they are from; I just smile and think they must be having a family gathering up there. This may not be something that works for everyone, but it sure works for me. It makes my day special if I find a penny or a dime. It always makes me smile, I always say "Hi Jeff" or "Hi Dad," and I always remember "In God We Trust", and I do.

> But I have noticed that during the most trying periods of my life there have only been one set of footprints in the sand. Why, when I needed you most, you have not been there for me? The Lord replied, "The times when you have seen only one set of footprints in the sand, is when I carried you."
>
> ~ Mary Stevenson

ANGEL NUMBERS...My Angel Number – 23

The number 23 has always been significant in my life and in the lives of both of my children. That being said, it was no surprise when the number 23 began appearing to me in many ways after losing my son. I could write an entire chapter on Angel numbers...maybe in my next book...if there is one! I have several three digit repeating Angel numbers all ending in 23, but for this book, I will elaborate on only the Angel number 23.

"The number 23 is made up of the energies and attributes of the number 2 and number 3. Number 2 resonates with duality and balance, diplomacy and co-operation, faith and trust, duty and service, and your Divine life purpose and soul mission. Number 3 brings its vibrations of joy and optimism, self-expression and creativity, expansion and growth, encouragement and assistance. This makes 23 a number of duality, charisma, and communication." (Walmasley).

I have found that all of the qualities tied to these numbers do, indeed, make life more fulfilling and joyful. I use the talents given to me by God to reach out to others, and as a result, I receive more blessings. I feel that often times, Jeff is sending me his approval on the efforts I make in his memory by sending these numbers to me.

"Angel number 23 is a message that the angels are assisting you with maintaining your faith and trust in the universe as you work diligently to manifest your highest desires and aspirations. When feeling doubt or fear ask your angels for help and guidance as they are with you always." (Walmasley).

As stated by Joanne Walmasley in her ongoing blog, Sacred Scribes, "Angel number 23 is a message encouraging you to use your natural abilities, talents and creativity to bring joy and happiness into your life and into that of others. Communicate honestly and openly with others, and strive to help others in your daily life. What you put out to the universe comes back to you, so keep a **positive attitude** and **optimistic outlook** to ensure that all in your life remains balanced and harmonious. The repeating Angel number 23 is a reminder that your angels are always available to support, guide and assist you - all you need to do is ask." (Walmasley).

I truly believe this to be true. Keeping a positive attitude as I go through life has helped me heal and find that I truly can continue to live with the unexpected twist in my life story. Though this is not where I wanted my life to go, it is what I have been dealt and it is up to me to make sure that I make it positive and find a way to honor Jeff's memory. These reoccurring numbers are my assurance from Jeff that he approves of the way I am choosing to continue living for both of us.

After losing a loved one, holding on to them while letting go, is very important and can be done in so many different ways. In this chapter, and in chapter 7 - Signs…Sent From Heaven, you have read about the ways I have found to keep my son present in my life. I have never been to a physic or a medium, and doubt I ever will, but I did find comfort when I found Joanne Walmasley's website about Angel numbers.

Information obtained and used with the author's permission. Joanne Walmasley- Sacred Scribes http://sacredscribesangelnumbers.blogspot.com/2011/06/angel-number-23.html

> "Angels help you pick up the necessary pieces of your life and leave the others behind."
> ~Unknown

CHAPTER 9

HANDMADE WITH LOVE...
MEMORIES PRESERVED

Covered In Memories...A Memory Quilt

Not long after losing my son Jeff, I thought about making a memory quilt using Jeff's t-shirts. Jeff was an avid Jimmy Buffett fan and had dozens of Buffett t-shirts. Jeff and his sister, Kim, had gone to 23 Jimmy Buffett concerts together and, of course, bought t-shirts every time. In addition to the concert shirts, Jeff bought Buffett t-shirts every summer when he went to the beach. "Thought about", are key words when it came to actually making a quilt from Jeff's shirts. Although I thought it would be such a wonderful quilt to have, I just couldn't bring myself to cut Jeff's t-shirts apart.

Two years had passed when I told my friend, Mary Parr, about my idea to make a memory quilt from Jeff's t-shirts. This particular day, we were sitting in the rocking chairs, on the porch at The Old Gray House like we often do, talking about Jeff and remembering the last time Jeff, Mary, and I sat there together. Mary knew Jeff very well and could picture him in his Buffett t-shirt, sitting on the porch that day in June of 2010. Mary is an avid quilter and absolutely loved the idea of making a memory quilt. I remember that day so well. I told Mary that I just didn't think I could cut Jeff's t-shirts apart. I shared with her that in my mind, cutting his shirts apart made me feel like I would be cutting Jeff out of my life. Mary listened intently as I talked about Jeff, the memory quilt, and my feelings of sadness about cutting into his shirts.

Then, it was Mary's turn to talk. She talked about Jeff, our summers at the beach, how happy he was, and the memories we made and treasured. She pointed out that while we were making these memories at the beach, Jeff would have been wearing those Jimmy Buffett t-shirts that he loved. Mary then said something to me that totally changed my way of thinking. She looked at me and said, "Honey, you need to think about this quilt in a different light. You won't be cutting Jeff out of your life; you will be able to wrap his love and all those memories around you." She also said, "When you're ready, I will help you." I told her I would think about it.

I left the Old Gray House that day and while driving home, Mary's words kept going through my mind. A few days later, I told Mary that I loved the idea of wrapping Jeff's love and memories around me and I was ready to make a memory quilt. Mary had to cut the first shirt for me, and yes I had a few tears, but I was able to continue with Mary's expert help. As I cut and worked on each t-shirt, my thoughts were totally on my son. I could see him in those shirts, smiling as we walked on the beach together. I remembered us crafting together in my workshop as he was creating his driftwood beach shacks. So many other wonderful memories came back to me as I continued to make quilt patches for my memory quilt. I will forever be thankful for Mary's words of wisdom and for encouraging me to make a beautiful quilt filled with memories of my son. Mary was right. When I use my quilt, I do feel Jeff's love and warmth surrounding me.

One night, not long after the quilt was finished, I had an amazing experience. It was a cold winter night, and I felt chilled after coming in from outdoors. I laid down on the sofa and grabbed the afghan that was beside me, but I just couldn't get warm. There was a second afghan on the back of the sofa that I pulled down on top of me. Still, I could not get warm. My husband picked up Jeff's memory quilt and put it over me. It was unbelievable - it was like Jeff's quilt was an electric blanket. Immediately, I felt warm once again. It was almost like that quilt was radiating heat. It was then that I truly believed that Mary was right – I was wrapping Jeff's memories, his love, and his warmth around me. I'm not sure if it's my imagination or if there really is a different kind of warmth that radiates from my memory quilt, but either way, I love the feeling of being able to wrap memories of my son around me.

I guess I'm like a child who carries her security blanket. My memory quilt travels with me to the beach house, and on every trip we take in our motor home. I love my quilt and my memories of Jeff that go with it.

Just A Memory Away

**I'm no longer by your side,
but there's no need to weep;**

I've left sweet recollections
I'm hoping you will keep.

Eternal joy and memories
stay in our hears forever,
Strengthening our special bond
that parting cannot sever.

Now it's time to journey on,
so let your faith be strong,
For I am in a better place...
I'm home where I belong.

And if times of loneliness
bring sorrow and dismay,
Don't despair, for I am there....
JUST A MEMORY AWAY.
~ Rita S. Beer

Memories...A Frog

I have come to the conclusion that memories of your loved one can be preserved in many ways. I would like to share a story about a frog I created in memory of my son Jeff.

My son received his first frog as a Christmas gift when he was two years old. He loved that little, stuffed frog and carried him everywhere and of course, had to sleep with him too. In the years that followed, Jeff was given more frogs, and by the time he was six, he decided he was going to collect those little critters. Jeff collected frogs all of his life, and a frog was always among his gifts at Christmas time. Remember, it was a frog that kicked Jeff's IV pole up a notch after his stem cell transplant.

In May, 2013, I went into a gift shop on Hatteras Island and the first item I noticed was a beautiful, jeweled frog, handcrafted by the owner of the shop. She used jewelry to create the frog and many other beautiful pieces of art. To me, it was spectacular and I absolutely loved her jeweled frog. As we chatted, I told her why her frog caught my eye. Although I could have purchased the frog she had made, she graciously offered to teach me how to make one of my own and suggested that I use some of my son's jewelry if I felt okay in doing so. I took her up on her offer to teach me the technique of jewelry art, and together, we created my special memory frog.

Having created my memory quilt using Jeff's t-shirts, I was okay with using his jewelry to create yet another keepsake. I used Jeff's Margaritaville watch face as the focal point of my frog. I had the pins Jeff earned in Boy Scouts and used one on each foot along with his Boy Scout arrow of light pin, his Elon College pin, and his Hope Lives On pin in my jeweled memory frog. The watch band was the base for the back legs of the frog, with the backs from the pins on top of it. The outline around the back legs was done with a necklace Jeff bought and wore at the beach. The four leaf clover was a gift to me from a good friend, and the cancer support pin belonged to me, and I wore it during the time Jeff was sick.

You'll also see other items that are meaningful to me - like angels, butterflies, crosses, and gemstones for July and September. July was Jeff's birth month and September is the month of his Angelversary. I love my little frog and will treasure him and all the memories that go with it forever.

This frog was made with some things my son left behind,
Things that have now become precious treasures of mine.
His watch and his pins that were tucked away in a drawer,
Now seen on my frog are these things that he wore.

This frog was made with jewels that
sparkle and gold that shines,
Will forever remind me of that son of mine.
When I gaze at this frog, I'll be reminded of love,
Love from my son who is now with God above.

~Sharon Crislip

Holding On While Letting Go

It can be very comforting to have special pieces made using your loved one's clothing, jewelry, or other mementos. I hope my memory quilt and my jeweled frog will inspire others to be creative when it comes to using items that belonged to your loved one; being creative with those special mementos is a great way to find comfort and keep their memory alive. There are many ways to keep our loved ones in our daily lives and keep their memory alive. My quilt and my frog do that for me. I hope you too find ways to be creative and preserve your precious memories.

CHAPTER 10

FRIENDS & FAMILY - OLD MEMORIES & NEW BEGINNINGS

Parents and Friends

My children, Kim and Jeff, are two of those lucky kids who have had four parents for many years. Kim was eleven, and Jeff was eight years old when I married Cris, which gave them two Dads – Arnold Crislip (Cris), and Denny Merrifield. Not long after that, Denny remarried giving Jeff two Moms – me, and Bonny Merrifield. Through the years, all four parents maintained a good relationship which of course was great for everyone. Denny and Bonny live in Pennsylvania, and we live in Virginia, so when Jeff was diagnosed with cancer in February 2006, being so far away was very difficult for Denny and Bonny. During Jeff's battle with cancer, Denny and Bonny visited regularly, but depended on Cris and me to keep them up to date when they weren't able to be in Virginia. We talked on the phone regularly until Jeff went into remission in October 2006. Life pretty much returned to normal while Jeff was in remission.

When Jeff's cancer returned in January of 2010, we all knew it was going to be a rough time. Denny and Bonny made several trips to Virginia to visit Jeff, and to also offer their support to Cris and me. Each time Denny and Bonny visited, I felt the relationship among the four of us was changing. Jeff's cancer created a bond among his four parents. We were all praying for a miracle, but by the end of the summer of 2010, we knew the situation was not good for Jeff. It was apparent Jeff could no longer be alone, so he came to live with Cris and me. This was a time when all four of Jeff's parents came together, not only as family, but also as friends. The four of us helped each other as we all tried to do everything we possibly could to make Jeff's last days with us as good as they possibly could be. Jeff was glad to have all four of his parents with him as he struggled to live. As Jeff was struggling, we too were struggling with seeing him in pain and knowing there was nothing we could do to take his pain away. It was during this time that Denny, Bonny, Cris, and I realized that we were not only parents, but we had indeed become friends. Having them with us to not only spend precious time with Jeff, but to spend time with us and help take care of our son, created a bond that I am certain will never change. To many people, it's strange that the four of us are friends - good friends, who enjoy spending time together. Even Jeff might be surprised at the friendship that developed.

We were always family because of our children, but now a very special friendship exists. Perhaps it is the fact that this friendship was born of desperation and despair, that it was forged in the fire of that awful time. We have lived the same battle; we have lost the same war. Today, we can reminisce about days gone by and remember our special old memories when we spend time together. It's a wonderful feeling to know that our friendship is a new beginning for all of us. Losing our son broke our hearts and our lives will never be the same without him, but it was our son who brought us together as friends. We have found strength in each other and peace in knowing that our son would be happy that his parents are family and friends, sharing old memories as we make new beginnings.

Dawn - A Special Person In My Life

You have read about the many signs I have received from my son so I'm sure you're not surprised when I tell you that I believe God put a very special young woman in my path for a reason. It was May 2013, a little more than two and a half years after losing my son, when I met Dawn.

I give credit to God, my Angel Jeff and to my Dad, and his Hometown Hero banner for bringing Dawn Gill into my life. I am certain Dawn also gives God credit along with her Angel Mom, Bea. The day I walked into the establishment Downtown Lock Haven, Inc., Dawn Gill greeted me with a beautiful smile and sparkling eyes. Instantly, I liked her. Dawn was responsible for creating banners for the Hometown Hero program. I had decided to have a banner created in memory of my Dad which led me to Dawn's office. I believe she could see how much I loved my Dad and how important this banner was to me. She worked diligently on my dad's banner – going above and beyond to make it perfect from an extremely old picture. I sat down beside Dawn as she worked on editing the picture. Since I am a person of many words who has never met a stranger, we began chatting.

During the next hour, Dawn and I both felt a connection. We felt that, just maybe, we were drawn to each other because of some really special people in our lives who now live in Heaven. I talked to Dawn about my son, Jeff, my daughter, Kim, my grandchildren, and of course my Dad. Dawn talked to me about her mom - Bea, and her daughter, Riley. During that hour I spent with Dawn while she was working on my Dad's banner, I could feel her kindness and her caring qualities. I knew we were kindred spirits. Dawn later told me she had the exact same feeling

During that hour, Dawn found out that my son, Jeff, went to Heaven at age forty. I found out that Dawn and Jeff were very close in age. She also learned that I was a Grandma who went overboard when it came to doing things for my grandchildren. I learned that Dawn's mother, who lost her life in a tragic car accident, did the same with her granddaughter, Riley, before she became one of God's Angels.

Holding On While Letting Go

As we continued our conversation, I mentioned to Dawn that we loved the Outer Banks and that we had a home at the beach in Avon, NC. Dawn then told me that her Mom had arranged a special family beach vacation, which as it turned out, was the last vacation she had with her entire family. The home they rented for their vacation was in Avon, NC – one mile from our home in Avon. The last special vacation Dawn had with her parents and sister was in a place where our family also loved to spend time together – another connection we share. We knew we wanted to spend more time together and learn more about each other's lives. Why?

For Dawn, the reason could have been that I reminded her of her Mom, which she said made her feel so good. For me, the reason could have been that Dawn's personality reminded me of Jeff. Her smile was contagious, and her eyes were caring, just like Jeff's. Dawn was touched and had tears in her eyes as I told her a few things about Jeff and the things that I do to keep his memory alive. It made me happy when she told me that she would like to start doing some of those same things in memory of her mother. I love talking about my son, and Dawn was willing to listen. Since that day, Dawn and I have become special friends, and we continue to discover many other things that we, and our Angels, have in common.

After spending more time together, we realized that Dawn's Mom – Bea, my son Jeff, and I all shared a love of Disney World. Dawn gave me a special gift as a thank you after I created a memory broach for her using her Mom's jewelry. I call these broaches AnJewels because they are made in the shape of an angel using pieces of jewelry. Dawn loves wearing her AnJewel, made with her Mom's jewelry, close to her heart and I loved making it for her.

Knowing I loved Disney as much as her Mom did, her thank you gift to me was her Mom's Disney watch. I can't begin to tell you how much it meant to me that Dawn would give me something that meant so much to her Mom. I love Bea's watch – which has already made two trips to Disney World with me. Dawn also gave me an ornament that she had purchased for her mom at Disney World. I looked at it and smiled – and also got chills. The ornament that Dawn had given me, purchased for her Mom, was the exact same ornament that Jeff had bought for me on one of his Disney trips. There are thousands of ornaments to choose from at Disney World. How is it that two children, hundreds of miles apart, who never met, chose the same ornament for their mothers? How is it that one child and one mother's lives would cross years later? Our Angels love of Disney would be the first of many things that Dawn and I would discover that we have in common.

As time passed we continued to discover things that are parallel in our lives. Dawn's mother collected snowmen – I also have a snowman collection. Dawn's mother loved Christmas - Christmas has always been my favorite holiday. Jeff and Dawn have that same humorous, but sarcastic attitude which I absolutely love. Something as simple as finding out that Dawn and Jeff both shared a love of chocolate cake with peanut butter icing and Jimmy Buffett makes me smile.

When I realized that Dawn lived one mile from my mother's home, I couldn't believe it. Not only is her home close to my mother's, the home that Dawn bought and now lives in was previously the home of my great aunt and uncle. Dawn's home was built by two of my great great uncles in the early 1900's. As you can see, it is clear that Dawn and I were destined to become friends. In a sense, I feel that our Angels put this meeting in motion to help us both deal with our respective losses.

I have learned many important life lessons since losing my son. One of those lessons is that God works in mysterious ways and puts people in our lives at just the right time. Dawn came into my life because I wanted to do something special in memory of my Dad, and we became friends in an instant. What I didn't know when I walked into her office was that she was leaving that job the following week. My Dad's banner was one of the last that she created. Yes, I believe God is the reason for our friendship - He knew Dawn needed a "Mom" and I needed a "child." Because of our losses, Dawn and I have found friendship that I am sure will last a lifetime. I believe our Angels knew we needed each other.

As I write this, it has been nearly two years since I met Dawn. I am truly blessed to have this wonderful young woman I think of as another daughter in my life. Dawn and her family have become very important to me and all because of a chance meeting. Coincidence? I don't think so. I believe all things happen for a reason and all in God's plan.

I am hoping that sharing this story will encourage those of you reading this to always be aware of new people who come into your life after the loss of a loved one. A smile and a few kind words to start a conversation could be the beginning of a wonderful friendship when you need it most.

> **There is a miracle called Friendship**
> **that dwells within the heart**
> **And you don't know how it happens**
> **or when it even starts.**
>
> **But the happiness it brings you**
> **always gives a special lift**
> **And you realize that Friendship**
> **is God's most precious gift.**
> ~Abby Garza

All In a Nights Chat…
~Sherri Breazeale

First of all, let me just say that my contribution to this book has been mainly to support my friend, Sharon, in fulfilling her promise to her son. I have been a sounding board, a brainstormer, an editor, and encourager. But, in all of that, my biggest part in all of this has been to be her friend. Amazingly, all of this was done through nightly Facebook chats and emails. We are the self-proclaimed "Queens of Chat!"

How do you become friends with someone who lives in a different state whom you have never met? How do you become lifelong friends even before you hear each other's voices? For Sharon and me, it was through mutual and much loved friends. You see, Sharon is always taking care of others. In this case, she was making sure that all the people who loved Mary and Dewey Parr, were kept informed and were praying for them through their own personal crisis. I returned a simple message on Facebook, thanking her for keeping us up to date on the situation, and she responded. Before we even knew what was happening, we were fast friends.

Holding On While Letting Go

Very early into our friendship, I asked Sharon to share Jeff's story with me. I was, at first, hesitant, not knowing how she would feel about this and knowing that it could be painful. Sharon immediately put me at ease and told me to ask anything that I wanted to. I soon found out that this was her way of keeping Jeff's memory alive. She wanted to share his story so it would give others hope that, like herself, they too could make it through the unimaginable and back into the light. She wanted to make sure that Jeff left a legacy to be proud of.

As our friendship grew, we continued our nightly chats. It is funny how much you can learn about someone over a chat, how much more you share and open up about. We began chatting in May of 2013 and were still getting to know each other when my husband and I made our yearly trip to the Outer Banks of North Carolina in June. The funny thing, Sharon and her hubby, Cris, own a beach house there and though we knew we were going to be that close, we made no plans to meet at that time because Sharon was having a house guest. The afternoon before we were to leave and head for home, I decided to go back to The Old Gray House and say goodbye to Mary and Dewey, our friends and the owners of the shop. As I walked in to see Mary, there were a couple of ladies standing at the counter. Nothing unusual, as the Gray House is a popular stop for many. I told Mary that I just popped in to say goodbye and she introduced me to the ladies at the counter. One of them was Sharon! Can I just say here, it truly is a small world! Our first face to face was brief, and as I am challenged at meeting new people, a bit awkward. I mean, I had shared so much with this woman…and this was the first time I had even heard her voice! Of course, that night we were once again burning up the chat lines!

Our friendship continued to blossom, and we continued our nightly chats. One night, when I signed on to Facebook, I saw that Sharon had posted pictures of a Christmas Workshop that Jeff had done for his nephews to help them get gifts for their family. Instantly, I had an "Aha" moment. You see, I am a teacher, and I was having one of "those" years.

Sharon A Crislip

You know the ones. The ones that make you wonder what you were thinking when you decided to become a teacher. Well, I was smack dab in the middle of one of "those" years and needed a way to encourage my more difficult students to want more for themselves, while also rewarding those kids that were doing their very best already. I used the idea of Jeff's Christmas Workshop as a foundation and built a classroom management plan around it. I told the kids about my friend, Sharon, and her son, Jeff. We talked about how he always tried to do his best to be the best person that he could, to help others who were in need, to reach for his dreams and to expect to be successful. I told them that they had to work hard for what they wanted and that it would be worth much more to them in the end. I told them how Ms. Sharon worked hard to make sure people remembered what a wonderful, kind man Mr. Jeff was. We discussed what we wanted people to think of when they think about each of us. Unbelievably, I got some very profound answers. This was resonating with the kids!

Once we determined what was important to our success in class and as a citizen in our school, I introduced the idea to them about earning tokens (or angel pennies as they call them) and using them to purchase snacks for themselves and save enough to buy gifts for their families at our very own Christmas workshop. This would become only the first Mr. Jeff's Merri-Filled Christmas Workshop (named of course, in honor of my inspiration for taking on this project, Jeff Merrifield). I ran this idea past Sharon, and she was all in. She was thrilled that I was using Jeff as a source of inspiration and allowing his work of mentoring his middle school students to continue. The results that we saw in our classroom were magical. No, the issues did not disappear, but they decreased. Students began to self-monitor in their efforts to build their token totals. I developed a punch card system that allowed them to easily see their progress, and of course, for a more immediate reinforcement, they were able to buy snacks from the classroom snack store with some of their tokens.

While this was, to the dreamers (Sharon and myself) a great idea, it would be an expensive endeavor for me. Just keeping snacks in stock for a middle school class is a daunting task and gathering gifts for a Christmas workshop was going to get expensive in a hurry. Once again, Jeff and Sharon to the rescue. Help came in many ways; of course, Sharon and I began to collect items to supply the shop, but we were also blessed with contributions of items from our own friends, Ms. Mary from the Old Gray House, and Jeff's friends and family. So many people helped bring this dreamed up plan to reality. Even the wrapping paper was donated to our project! There was no doubt, the way everything was falling into place, that this "idea" was not just a coincidence. Jeff's idea was there waiting for me to find it, and God made sure I did!

Finally, December arrived, and with it, the date for the first Mr. Jeff's Merri-Filled Christmas Workshop, and even better…the arrival of Cris and Sharon! There was NO WAY that this workshop was going to happen without them! The workshop was a huge success. Gifts were bought for moms, dads, brothers, sisters, grandparents, aunts, uncles, pets, and one another. Best of all, the kids finally got to give a very special project they had been involved in to Ms. Sharon. My mother, being an amazingly talented and creative woman, had come to my classroom and helped the kids make individual quilt blocks. We also added blocks that Mom and I embroidered with very special symbols and signs that represent Jeff to Sharon. Even the hardest middle school tough guys were touched and shed a few tears seeing her reaction to their gift. I was thrilled to see the kids learn to look beyond themselves and think about others. They were so very thoughtful in putting together their surprise for Sharon, and in choosing gifts for their families.

So there you have it. This is how two people who had never met can become lifelong friends, and book collaborators, all in a night's chat...well, ok, many a night's chat. Sharon and I have discussed this many times in our brainstorming sessions, and our only explanation is that Jeff decided we needed each other. It seems odd, indeed, to think back and realize that we had been friends for such a short time. There was an instant connection between Sharon and Cris and my hubby and me. There have been many fun times and adventures together since, and more are being planned. It seems that things are exactly as they were always meant to be. For me, I believe that there is truly nothing left to chance. All is done in God's plan, in His timing. I am thankful that God decided to put me in the path to find Jeff's story, and through it, some very dear friends. Life is richer with friendships...even if they are made "all in a night's chat!"

I will pick up where Sherri left off. A lot has happened because of what started "all in a night's chat" on Facebook. Early in 2013, I posted pictures on Facebook that I had found of "Santa's Workshop" at Jeff's house along with a list of jobs that his nephews and niece could do to earn tokens to spend at this workshop to buy Christmas gifts for their family. Jeff's Santa's Workshop was such a fun time for the kids and for Jeff, Cris, and me. It was also fun for Robin and Mina Simler who were Jeff's gift wrapping elves!! Little did I know that posting those pictures on Facebook would lead to this event being recreated by a special friend of mine. My friend, Sherri, is a teacher in Tennessee, who teaches some very special children, indeed! Her students, like all children these days, are trying to find their way in this world of broken homes and hard knocks. Often times, they are just looking for someone to love them and be a role model for them. She was inspired by Jeff's Santa's Workshop idea to do something special for her students.

Sherri has touched my heart in a way that I will never forget. She used Jeff's story and the way he lived his life as a learning experience for her students. Her goal is to teach them to be confident, to have courage to tackle difficulties in life, to always try to help others, to think positively and to use Jeff as a much needed role model for her students. She asked me to write a letter, Jeff's story so to speak, so she could introduce Jeff to her students, which of course I was excited to do. I sent Sherri the letter and Jeff was introduced to her students.

During our many chats, Sherri said some things that helped to heal my heart. I have learned that kind words shared by others about my son were a crucial part of my grief process. Moving forward after your loss is difficult to say the least. As you read some of the messages sent to me by Sherri, and the reactions of her students, try to imagine the importance of these words to a mother who lost her only son.

Sherri wrote:

"I plan to share Jeff's story with the kids and tell them that the workshop is his idea, passed to me by his mother, who misses him very much. I will also be telling them that it is important to live a life that, no matter what happens

in the future, will continue to show people how important it is to do good and to help others. I sincerely believe that Jeff continues to prosper and will influence the lives of others far beyond what we can imagine. I never met the man, and he is influencing mine and how I reach out to others. Jeff is such an inspiration and a remarkable role model. Because of circumstances beyond their own control, often times children are lacking a role model, either male or female, from their lives. While I can be that female role model, middle school boys need a positive male influence during this this time of their lives when so much of what they learn about how to become independent, kind, successful men occurs."

Sherri wrote:

"My kids need quality male role models in their lives. Jeff and the way he lived life will serve to fulfill this need. The kids are already talking about next year's workshop, so you see, it is already growing! I think that using Jeff as a model for the kids and by allowing them to take ownership of the workshop, help set up, organize, work it, and learn about Jeff's story in the process will show them responsibility and that they too can learn to be like Jeff. I feel certain they will like the idea and it will continue to grow and spread."

"I introduced my kids to Mr. Jeff, and they had all kinds of questions. They wanted to know if I had met him. I told them, "No, but he is a very special friend on Facebook and is extra special because he is helping me find ways to be a good teacher to you." They asked if his mom was still sad, and I said "Of course, but she looks for butterflies and pennies and knows that when she finds them, he is watching over her." We went on a walk around the campus looking for pennies and they were so excited to find two, side by side. One of the kids said, "I bet that is Mr. Jeff and his Mom talking to each other. We picked them up and put them up in a special box on my desk. The coolest thing happened the next morning, when the kids came in from their buses. Two different kids had gone home and looked all over their houses and brought in handfuls of pennies!!!! They asked if I would keep them and give them to Mr. Jeff's mom. These two kids are opposite ends of the spectrum...one sweet, precious little

dainty girl in 6th grade (probably weighs 60 lbs. soaking wet) and one of my 8th grade tough guys!"

"When we talked about Jeff and Mr. Jeff's Merri-Filled Christmas Workshop, the kids were so excited. They talked and talked about Mr. Jeff and how nice he was! Needless to say, Mr. Jeff is very popular with my kids. When I gave them their morning break, one of the kids found a huge plastic silver penny that I didn't even know we had and yelled across the room, "I found an ANGEL PENNY"! She was so excited! I have attached pictures of the pennies the kids brought in this morning, the silver angel penny, and the two pennies we found on the campus. About the handfuls of pennies the two students brought in...I was so touched and so proud! I love especially that my "tough guy" was willing to share his heart."

Sherri continues: *"I have been trying to figure out where to go from here and this is what I thought...we talked about how Jeff liked to help people, so I want them to see that they can do the same thing for people even though they don't have money. So...we are going to be bucket fillers and every time they perform a kindness for someone, they will earn an Angel penny to add to their buckets. They will also earn pennies for doing kind things for themselves...studying for their spelling test and making a passing grade (which is so hard for most of them), not giving up when something is really hard, trying even when they are afraid they will get the answer wrong, starting the day "over" when they have really messed up and had an ugly attitude...I think it is really going to help them build confidence and character!"*

"Mr. Jeff's Merri-Filled Christmas Workshop is for the kids and Jeff's legacy...Jeff's legacy because of the way you have inspired me in your grief, and then Jeff himself through his story that you shared with me. The biggest reason is to make a difference for those kids. I'll tell you, Sharon, I have seen children go to the "school-wide" Santa's Workshop for four years now and look - look because that was all they could do, and wish they could shop. Even before I was teaching, I would go with my own kids to let them shop, and there were always those students who were unable to buy gifts because they had no money. I have

seen how excited they get when their day to go arrives, and I have watched them walk out without anything...over and over and over. Yes, we have made gifts to try to take the place of buying, but you know how exciting it is for kids to shop and pick out gifts for others. I would never have thought to take it all on and do a Santa's Workshop ourselves without those pictures you posted of Jeff's Santa's Workshop for his nephews." Earning Angel tokens to shop at Mr. Jeff's Workshop will make it possible for my kids to purchase gifts for their families.

During his 17 year career at Beville Middle School, Jeff was a role model for many students. He always had time to listen, to help, to encourage, and to laugh with "his kids." And now, Jeff will continue to be a role model for young people as my friend Sherri shares Jeff's life's story with her students. Not long before Jeff left this earth, he made a comment to his best friend, Ben Riley, that he was going to die without making a mark on this world. I hope Jeff knows that he did make a difference and he did leave a mark on this world. Jeff's legacy lives on and he continues to help and inspire people, young and old alike, not only through Mr. Merrifield's Mitten Trees at Beville Middle School in Dale City, VA and Mountain View High School in Stafford, VA, (more on the mitten trees in another chapter) but now through Mr. Jeff's Merri-Filled Christmas Workshop in Tennessee. This has become an annual event, and each year the students continue to be excited, earn their "Angel pennies," and remember Mr. Jeff in a very special way.

> ## "Coincidence is God's way of remaining anonymous"
> ~Albert Einstein

CHAPTER 11

HIS LEGACY LIVES ON....

A couple months before Jeff became my Angel, he made a comment to his best friend, Ben Riley, which almost broke my heart. I didn't find out until after Jeff was gone, but the comment he made to Ben was that he was upset because he was probably going to die without having made his mark in this world. I hope he knows that he truly has made his mark in this world and has inspired many, many people to continue to do the things, in his memory, that meant so much to him when he was alive.

Mr. Merrifield's Mitten Tree
For 17 years while Jeff worked at Beville Middle School, his yearly project was to do a mitten tree at Christmas time. He put up a Christmas tree in the cafeteria at his school and had a challenge between the students and the teachers. The challenge was bringing in mittens, hats, and scarves to decorate the tree - all of which would be donated to homeless shelters in our area. Jeff volunteered to be the designated shopper for the teachers who didn't have time to fit shopping for mittens, hats, and scarves into their hectic schedule. Every year, he sent an email to the teachers letting them know if they wanted to give him cash donations, he would do all the shopping for them. The teachers loved having a personal shopper, and Jeff was an avid shopper and was always looking for good sales so he could get the most for the money. Jeff also offered incentives to the kids during this challenge. I remember one of the incentives he used – he told the students that bringing in mittens to keep needy children warm made him smile, and anyone who made him smile

would get a mini Snickers candy bar when they brought in their items. Every year, many children - and adults were a little bit warmer in the winter because of Jeff's efforts and dedication to the mitten tree project.

Jeff lost his battle with cancer on Sept. 23, 2010, but Jeff's Mitten Tree tradition lives on. The bookkeeper at Jeff's school, Lori Brickley, is a very good friend of mine since we held the same position for many years - she at Beville Middle School, and me at Godwin Middle School. Lori called me in October of that year and told me they were going to continue with Jeff's Mitten Tree and asked me if I would like to help. Of course I wanted to help - and volunteered to be the designated shopper just like Jeff was. I then posted on Facebook and sent an email to all my friends and family telling them if they wanted to help make Jeff's Mitten Tree bigger and better than ever by donating a pair of mittens, a hat, or a scarf, to drop them in the mail to me - or send them to the school. The response was overwhelming and beautiful. We had to put up two additional trees. There were over 1000 items to be donated to those in need - it was absolutely amazing.

A second Merrifield Mitten Tree was started in 2011 by a teacher who had worked with Jeff and loved the Mitten Tree project. She left his school and moved to another county to teach and wanted to start a Mitten Tree at her new school. She contacted me, letting me know what she was going to do, and since Jeff always took care of taking the items from the Mitten Tree to the shelters, she hoped I knew where the items could be donated. She has had "Mr. Merrifield's Mitten Tree" at her school every year since 2011, and she uses Jeff's story as a teaching experience for her students. All she knew was Jeff did the tree but didn't know all the ins and outs of getting it all together and making sure the items got to the homeless shelters. I gave her all the info, and she invited us to the holiday party she had for her students, so we could see all the mittens on their tree. The tree was brimming over with mittens, hats, and scarves. She continues to do Mr. Merrifield's Mitten Tree at her school and The Merrifield Mitten Tree tradition continues every year at Jeff's school too. Many children are warmer in the winter as Jeff's legacy lives on.

The Merrifield Café

In December of 2011, a special ceremony was held at Beville Middle School to honor Jeff's 17 years of working there. During those years, Jeff had made a huge difference in the lives of many students who were heading down the wrong path in life. The administration and staff prepared the proper paperwork to be presented to the school board to request permission to rename and dedicate the school cafeteria in memory of Jeff. The cafeteria was chosen because Jeff spent three hours of his day in the cafeteria during lunch shifts. Jeff believed that if you were going to help children, you needed to know them. Where better to get to know children and talk to them than during their lunch break? The kids trusted Jeff, looked up to him, and valued his advice. Part of Jeff's job, as a security specialist, was to help maintain a safe environment for the students and staff. Spending time in the cafeteria, and getting to know the students outside of the classroom setting enabled Jeff to "head off" potential behavior problems. He always said it's amazing what kids will tell you, to try to help avoid a problem, when you earn their trust.

One of the students that Jeff helped in middle school, and most likely met for the first time in the cafeteria, came to me at his funeral because she had something she wanted me to know. This young lady was then a senior in high school. She told me that if it hadn't been for Mr. Merrifield, she wouldn't be on the path she is on in high school. She told me that she wasn't exactly a good student in middle school, and Mr. Merrifield got her back on the right track more than one time. She told me that Mr. Merrifield was never too busy to listen, and he always took time to help set her straight. She said thanks to Mr. Merrifield, she was a straight A student and on her way to college. I can't tell you how much her words meant to me. I can't say for sure, but I'm guessing that some of Jeff's words of wisdom to this young lady took place in the cafeteria at Beville Middle School.

The cafeteria was dedicated to Jeffrey Merrifield and renamed "The Merrifield Café."

Holding On While Letting Go

Mr. Jeff's Merri-Filled Christmas Workshop

You have read about this very special event in another chapter – "All In A Night's Chat…" so I won't go into all the details of Mr. Jeff's Merri-Filled Christmas Workshop again. The Christmas Workshop has become an annual event at Pigeon Forge Middle School. During his 17 year career at Beville Middle School, Jeff was a role model for many students. He always had time to listen, to help, to encourage, and to laugh with "his kids". And now, Jeff will continue to be a role model for young people as Sherri shares his life's story with her students. As I wrote in the beginning of this chapter, Jeff commented to his best friend that he was going to die without making a mark on this world. As you can see, Jeff did make a difference and he did leave a mark on this world. Jeff's legacy lives on and he continues to help and inspire people, young and old alike, not only through Mr. Merrifield's Mitten Trees at Beville Middle School in Dale City, VA and Mountain View High School in Stafford, VA, but also through Mr. Jeff's Merri-Filled Christmas Workshop in Pigeon Forge, Tennessee. Jeff will be remembered, in a special way, every year by these children when they attend Mr. Jeff's Merri-Filled Christmas Workshop.

As his mother, my heart is overjoyed with everything that is being done in my son's memory. As these events continue, I really realize just how much of an inspiration Jeff was, and is, to so many people. It's truly amazing. I just want so badly to know that Jeff knows he really did make a mark in this world. His inspirations going to Tennessee to help children – he would be so happy to know he is still making a difference to young people. I am excited and proud that a very special teacher in Tennessee is honoring Jeff's memory and sharing his story with her class. You will read the details about Mr. Jeff's Merri-Filled Christmas Workshop in another the chapter Friends & Family…Old Memories & New Beginnings.

Birthday Basket for a Baby

I continually try to find new ideas or projects to keep Jeff's memory alive so his legacy will continue to live on for as long as I am on this earth. Another way I make this happen is with a birthday basket for a new born baby – a baby born on Jeff's birthday. I fill a basket with baby gifts, and take the basket to our local hospital to be given to a baby born on July 23rd. The first year I took the basket to the hospital, the parents of the baby the basket was given to allowed me to visit with them and hold their newborn son. When the baby's father placed his son in my arms, my eyes filled with tears and my heart was overjoyed as I held this new little boy and reflected on the little boy I held in my arms on July 23rd forty one years ago. It was an amazing feeling and a day I will remember forever. Hospital security with babies has changed since then, so I no longer get to meet the parents and baby, but I include a card with the gift letting them know that my son is now an Angel and thanking them for allowing me to celebrate my son's life by sharing gifts with their newborn child who was born on his birthday.

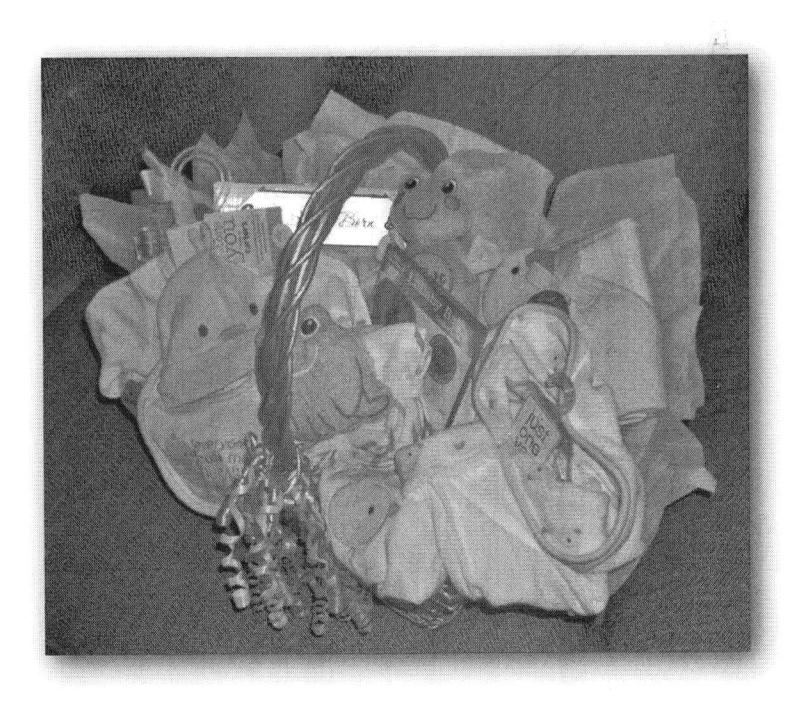

Adopt A Classroom

I am adding this paragraph totally at the last minute – the evening before I send my manuscript off to the publisher, and one day after my son's

45th birthday. Because security has become an issue at many hospitals when it comes to newborns, I decided I needed a backup plan for giving gifts on Jeff's birthday. I'm not giving up on the baby basket idea, but must find a better way to make it possible to give the basket of gifts to a baby born on Jeff's birthday. Hence, a new plan was born! On my son's birthday – July 23, 2015 – I decided to adopt a classroom and purchase school supplies for children in need. It seemed like the perfect project since Jeff worked for the school system for seventeen years and loved helping children. I spent the afternoon, on his birthday, shopping for back to school supplies, smiling and "talking" to Jeff as I was making decisions on what to buy. I had fun buying "birthday gifts" and I feel certain Jeff approved since there was a bright, shiny 2015 Angel penny on the floor waiting for me as I entered the checkout line. This birthday box, full of back to school supplies, will make its way to the classroom I adopted, and a classroom full of children will have the supplies they need to start their new school year.

Angel Gowns - NICU Helping Hands

In my search for ways to do things in memory of my son, I learned about a group called "NICU Helping Hands". This non-profit organization has a program called The Angel Gown Program. Volunteer seamstresses create beautiful gowns for babies who never go home from the Neonatal Intensive Care Unit. They make these gowns from donated wedding gowns. When I heard about this program, I immediately wanted to be a part of it.

Every year, I do something special on Jeff's Angelversary – September 23rd, the anniversary of the day Jeff became an Angel. September 23rd will always be a special day that will be forever shared by both of my children; it is the day that Jeff became an Angel, it is also my daughter Kim's birthday

September 23, 2014, Jeff's fourth Angelversary, and Kim's forty seventh birthday, Kim and I spent the day shopping for wedding gowns. It's hard, as a Mom, to try and get through both of these events on the same day, but with faith and God's help, I am able to do it. We started our day at the Cracker Barrel Restaurant by having Jeff's favorite breakfast, "Eggs in the Basket". As we entered the Cracker Barrel, I found four Angel pennies laying side by side, one for each year Jeff had been our Angel. At that point, Kim and I were sure Jeff was with us. After breakfast, we began our trek to the Goodwill stores to look for wedding gowns. Our goal was to find four gowns, one for each year Jeff had been in Heaven – and we did just that. The four wedding gowns we bought were beautiful and we knew they would make gorgeous "Angel gowns" for precious little babies to wear when they went to Heaven.

To quote NICU Helping Hands – "There is no greater gift that can be given to a grieving family than affirming the importance of the life of their child by offering the simple gift of our Angel Gown® and supporting them emotionally and educationally afterwards."

If you would like to participate in the Angel Gown program, in memory of your loved one, by donating wedding gowns, or volunteering to be one of their seamstresses, you can find the information you need at the following website:

http://www.nicuhelpinghands.org/lend-a-helping-hand/angel-gowns/

Project Night Night...Helping homeless children have sweeter dreams

Jeff always loved helping children in need, so when I discovered Project Night Night, I again knew this was something I wanted to do in Jeff's memory. They donate Night Night packages each year to homeless children, age twelve and under, who need childhood essentials to help them have a concrete source of security and an increased exposure to literacy materials during a time of upheaval in their lives. Each Night Night package contains a new security blanket, an age-appropriate children's book, and a stuffed animal - all nestled inside of a new canvas tote bag. Every child who receives a Night Night Package leaves the homeless shelter owning a book which encourages reading and family bonding, a security blanket which can be cuddled, and a stuffed animal which can become a cherished friend. The hope is to give homeless children something they can call their own, something that can give them that little bit of comfort and confidence to be able to deal with what lies ahead of them. Knowing this is a project Jeff would have loved to be a part of, I decided Project Night Night is another perfect way to keep Jeff's legacy alive.

Information on how you can participate in Project Night Night, in memory of your loved one can be found at the following website:

http://www.projectnightnight.org/

Jeff's Star – International Star Registry

Because Jeff was my shining star throughout his battle, I decided he really did need a star of his own. I had heard about the International Star Registry and just had to see if I could indeed dedicate a star to my son. I was so happy that I was able to purchase a star – Jeff's very own star and have it registered in the International Star Registry. His star is named Jeff Merrifield and the date of dedication is September 23, 2010 – the day he became our Angel. The telescopic coordinates of Jeff's star are Ursa Major RA 12h 2m 17.47s D39 5' 8.89". Fortunately, for those of us who aren't scientific, they also send a location map which enabled us to easily find Jeff's star. What an amazing feeling it is to look at the sky and know my son has his very own star. I may not always focus on exactly the right star when I look to the night sky, but to me, Jeff can be any one of those beautiful stars in the sky. Just knowing he has a beautiful star named after him and dedicated to him is what warms my heart.

If you would like to have a star named in memory of your loved one, you can find the information on the International Star Registry at the following website:

http://www.starregistry.com/

In this chapter, I have written about many different ideas and projects that have given me comfort, and kept my mind occupied along my journey through the grief of losing my son. The joy of giving to others, while keeping Jeff's memory alive, is a wonderful feeling. I find hope I have inspired you to try some of my ideas to keep your loved ones memory alive in your heart and in the hearts of others. I am still on my grief journey and will continue to try and find new, projects to do in Jeff's memory. One of the goals in my life is to make sure Jeff's legacy lives on.

I would like to end this portion of the book with two very special notes.

Five days before Jeff went home to be with God, I received a message from one of Jeff's cousins - Lori Flanigan Ziemba. As I read Lori's message, I had tears in my eyes reading how she felt and what she learned from Jeff. I shared her words with Jeff and they meant the world to him.

Lori wrote:

The strength and faith Jeff has in fighting this battle is nothing short of amazing. He has spoken to us all as a motivational speaker. He may not be standing in front of a podium, but we have all learned so much from him already.

I have learned to put my faith in God for strength in all things. I have learned that the human mind, spirit and body have a strength beyond belief. I have learned that family is the center of all things important. I have learned to cherish every moment with the ones I love. I have learned that humor helps feed the mind and body. I have learned that the power of prayer does amazing things. I have learned that the support of family and friends gives us comfort and peace. Above all, I have learned to cherish the gifts in my life - the gifts of faith, family, friends, and health.

So, I just wanted Jeff to know that his motivational speech has been going on for years and I have heard and been changed by it. Thank you Jeff. We love you for all you have been through for the lessons we have all learned. Keep the faith, and you will continue to inspire us!! Love, Lori

After I lost my son, a dear friend of mine, Dewey Parr (my Beach Dad), wrote to me and shared his feelings about how he felt about Jeff.

Dewey wrote:
It is hard for me to put in words the feeling in my heart concerning the loss of your son, Jeff. Jeff was like the lighthouse to me. When I was growing up on Hatteras Island, the symbol of hope, security, and strength was the light from our mighty lighthouse shining at night over the Island. At night I would lay with my head in the window from my bedroom in our little house on the Buxton Front Road and watch the flickering of the light in the dark sky. Many a night I fell asleep with the feeling all was well because the light was still shining. As I watched Jeff deal with his battle with cancer, I had the same feeling. I only hope that when my time comes I can be as positive and strong and put out rays of hope and joy to those around me like Jeff did. In my heart, Jeff will never be forgotten, for every time I look at the lighthouse or see its rays in the night sky over my house he will be in my thoughts. Jeff was and still is my shining light in the darkness. Jeff has been a shining light to many people.

In my heart I truly believe that Lori's words showed Jeff that he really did make a mark on this world, and Dewey's words showed me that my son really was a shining star in his battle with cancer and that he did leave a legacy that would live on.

> People are like stained-glass windows. They sparkle and shine when the sun is out, but when the darkness sets in their true beauty is revealed only if there is light from within."
> ~Elisabeth Kübler-Ross

CHAPTER 12

HIS SISTER REMEMBERS....

As I continued to write and finish the book that Jeff had started, it occurred to me that Jeff's sister, Kim, had memories of her brother that she might like to share. You will read Jeff's Story at the end of this book in the Epilogue, but the memories his sister will share will let you know Jeff as a brother and an uncle.

Kim writes:

By this point in the book, you have met my brother, Jeff, and have gotten to know him from his own writings and also as a son from the chapters written by my mother. I want to share the Jeff I knew as a brother and as an uncle to my children. I won't get into all my sadness and loss, that isn't how Jeff was to me. I want you to meet my brother through some of the happiest moments we shared.

Jeff and I were siblings – exactly 2 years and 10 months apart. I was born on September 23, 1967, and Jeff arrived on July 23, 1970. Imagine that, both of us born on the 23rd. Little did we know that in the years to follow, the number 23 would have significant meaning. I wish I could say I remembered the day I became a big sister, but that's a stretch for an almost three year old. I'm sure I was a huge help to our parents, but I must say, I was a bit of a handful growing up. My parents tell me I went kicking and screaming to that first day of kindergarten, and I remember clearly doing the same thing until I graduated from high school. Jeff, on the other hand, loved school – a concept I could not understand. I just knew that Jeff's brain needed rewired; why would you come home from school and do homework when the great outdoors awaited us? Jeff's liking for school and education just didn't seem normal to me. I knew something was clearly wrong with this boy. I felt the need, in our younger years, to change Jeff. His failure to conform to my standards would be the cause of some major childhood battles. It became clear from an early age that Jeff was just plain different.

Our younger years were spent in the mountains of Pennsylvania. Neighbors were few and far between. Pennsylvania was a place where your playmates were your cousins; your babysitters were your grandparents, aunts and uncles. Jeff and I weren't always friends. Remember I told you there was something wrong with that boy. However, we learned at an early age that we had something in common. Yes, Jeff and I were bilingual. We were fluent in both English and sarcasm. When people who were not bilingual like us were the objects of our sarcasm, we found it hysterical. BUT – when our gift of sarcasm was used on each other, many times it required our parents to separate us. Let's just say we got carried away with that sibling rivalry.

Fast forward five years. Our parents divorced. Two years later when Mom was going to remarry, we were told we would be moving to Virginia. Virginia I thought? Where in the world is that? Doesn't everyone alive live in Lock Haven, Pennsylvania? Jeff informed me that Virginia was in the south. The south, where was that? I was totally confused. The sad thing is by this point, I was in the fourth grade and Jeff was in first grade when he enlightened me about the state of Virginia. Go figure, that boy and his brain – I obviously didn't pay attention to geography in school. The summer before we moved, Mom informs us that there was year round school in Virginia. I was horrified, but Jeff was happy? Absolutely! Once again my suspicions were confirmed, something was wrong with that boy. We made the move to Dale City, Virginia. We moved into a townhouse, something Jeff and I had never seen before. Houses attached to one another, this was crazy and a culture shock. Homes stuck together, going to school for forty five days and then having fifteen days off all year round – what has our mom gotten us into? I quickly came to realize this was not so terrible. You see, when we were still too young to be left alone, we got to spend our fifteen days off in Pennsylvania. There, back home playing with our cousins, we weren't different; we didn't stand out from the other kids, but the jury was still out about Virginia. Jeff and I liked building forts and playing with his matchbox cars in the dirt roads in central Pennsylvania. We spent hours constructing roads and playing with his Tonka trucks. Jeff's toys were cool to me. I remember begging Jeff to let me drive that Tonka Winnebago RV. He wanted me to play with the little people. Dolls, I thought, never! Then before you know it, Jeff got that Stretch Armstrong doll - a doll we played tug of war with. The ultimate tomboy playing with Stretch Armstrong with her brother; I was happy, he was happy. Since I forced myself upon Jeff's toys, I decided he could play with my Lite Bright and Etch-A-Sketch.

I don't remember how long we lived in that townhouse, but I was sure happy when we moved into the house that would be our home for many years. When we moved to our new home, Mom and Dad's bedroom was on the main level, and Jeff and I had bedrooms upstairs. Our Mom was set in her ways, so of course Jeff and I had bedtimes. My mind, many nights, would not turn off. Jeff and I would tip toe into each other's rooms and quietly play Go Fish or War. If we thought we had been heard moving around upstairs, we knew how to play it off - flush the toilet. After all, we weren't hurting anything by staying up an extra 30 minutes. We felt accomplished.

Jeff also served his classmates when he was in the School Safety Patrol Program; he had that orange belt and silver badge. I was jealous – I never got to "officially" wear a school safety patrol belt. No, I had to wait for Jeff to go to sleep, then sneak into his room and take that patrol belt off his dresser. I would go into the bathroom and put on that belt all the while thinking I was really cool. When I was finished, I would wrap the belt up exactly like Jeff had it and set it back on his dresser. His safety patrol belt and mediator status started to over inflate that smart brain of his. The truth is, Jeff worked hard at school, and he deserved to be a safety patrol and a mediator. I was just plain jealous. I struggled with school while Jeff soared. I suppose this is the point in my chapter where I should admit to calling him a geek and a nerd. He would blurt back that I was a freak. I often told Jeff that in middle school, freaks beat up geeks, but that didn't deter Jeff and his love of school.

Those teenage years were soon upon us. Funny how things change. Jeff usually played with the younger crowd in our neighborhood while I played with kids who were my own age. However, there were days when we would all end up playing kick ball, whiffle ball, or dodge ball. It was then that Jeff became a little bit of a tattle tale. As usual, kids were kids, and at times arguments would occur, and I could never back down from a fight. Jeff would rush home to announce that I was fighting. Jeff tried to mediate, but I rarely listened. In fact, when Jeff was in fourth and fifth grade, he was a mediator at school. He did great mediating his peers, but he just couldn't get anywhere with me during those neighborhood arguments.

Moving forward to high school when I was a senior and Jeff was a freshman. I drove Jeff to and from school because there was no way I wanted my geeky kid brother on that school bus. That big yellow twinkie was not a place for a geek. I was in with my own elite group of friends during my junior and senior years of high school. I joined the fire department when I was sixteen years old and gave up my freak status to do something I loved. After twelve years of struggling through all those tests in school, I passed the firefighter classes and EMT classes with flying colors. After all those years in school thinking of Jeff as my intelligent kid brother, I discovered I, too, could earn A's on tests! Jeff seemed really proud of me and that made me happy. I would talk to him about the thrill of fighting a fire and the rush that came from flying down the roads on a fire truck or an ambulance. Jeff seemed to like hearing about my experiences in the fire department which encouraged me to continue in the field of being a first responder. Little did I know that Jeff's encouragement to help others would one day result in my becoming a nurse. But for now, I had found a trade I loved and saw no need to pursue higher education. Jeff, on the other hand, knew he was college bound.

Jeff and I chose very different paths in our lives. I graduated from high school and continued my studies and career as a firefighter and an EMT. Jeff was off to Elon College after his high school graduation to study Business Administration and Psychology. For the next four years, Jeff was at Elon College, in North Carolina, and I had relocated to Naples, Florida where my fiancé was employed as a fire chief. Although we were miles apart, we remained close and frequently shared stories by phone. Yes, I said by phone, an actual land line phone – no cell phones in the early 1990's, and no Facebook back then either! Jeff and I developed a real friendship during these years.

My fiancé and I moved back home to Virginia, married, and started our family. Jeff was nearing his college graduation and preparing to move back home as well. His goal after graduation was to go full speed ahead into the business world. However a college party resulted in Jeff breaking his leg. X-rays showed he not only had broken his femur, but there was also a tumor just above his knee. It was then that Jeff received his first cancer diagnosis, and his life's path would be changed forever.

Jeff graduated from Elon College in a special ceremony held by his college friends and one of his professors. The ceremony took place at Duke University Medical Center with Jeff receiving his diploma in his hospital bed. Jeff did wear a cap and gown when he graduated – college cap and hospital gown. His leg was in traction as he waited on the results of the tumor biopsy so needless to say his college graduation was slightly different than we had planned. You will read more about Jeff's first cancer diagnosis, in the chapter entitled Jeff's Story.

Holding On While Letting Go

Jeff and I had now entered the adult world. I am the mother of a son, Trey born in October 1991. Jeff was smitten with his nephew and gave in to the fact that he would no longer be the only "best looking guy in the family. Finally, there was someone else to help carry the burden of being the best looking person in our family. As the years went on, Jeff and Trey carried this vanity thing to the extreme, but it was fun, and to be honest, they were both very handsome young men. It was true; my brother absolutely was vain as well as humorously sarcastic.

Three years after Trey's birth, I gave birth to another son, Matthew. After Jeff's first bout with cancer in 1992, while he was recuperating, he took up a hobby – woodworking. Jeff decided to try his skills by making a wooden cradle. He finished the cradle just before Matthew was born. I was so proud to have a cradle made by my brother for my son to sleep in. Since Jeff worked less than a mile from my home, he frequently came by on his way home from work to spoil both his nephews. Those boys loved their Uncle Jeff, and he loved them. Jeff treated my boys as if they were his own. Fast forward four years, and my son Tony was born. Time to get that cradle out once again.

Tony's birth was special so to speak. My labor went on for 36 hours when suddenly the time arrived for this boy to be born. What I didn't realize was that the door to the birthing room was blocked by hospital personnel and, my Dad and brother were trapped inside the birthing room. No time to do anything but birth that baby with my husband, my Dad, and my brother in the room. Jeff really wanted to take pictures, but he ended up sitting in the corner on the sofa. My husband, Norman, my Dad and Jeff were watching the nurses take care of Tony, and Jeff finally got to take his pictures. Tony was now bundled up in his cute little hospital blanket when the nurse turned and saw three men standing there keeping watch. The nurse asked which one was the father, and my Dad popped off with "We won't know that until the blood test comes in." The nurse, in dismay, looked at me, and I confirmed that the tall man with curly hair was indeed Tony's father. Jeff and I laughed so hard we had tears in our eyes. Jeff returned to the sofa, with his snacks in hand as I began nursing Tony. Jeff, eating a powdered donut, his mouth full with sugary powder all over his lips, realized what was happening when Tony was under that blanket, he said "Hey Kim – got milk?" Jeff rarely missed the opportunity to bring humor into whatever was going on. Jeff now had three nephews to spoil, and that he did, always treating them as his own children. That continued until the day Jeff went to Heaven.

Jeff and I became closer in our adulthood years. We had many of the same friends, and we shared similar interests. Jeff claimed that he came to my house nearly every weekday for a cup of coffee before driving home from work, but I knew the real reason – he wanted to see his nephews. Jeff and I liked our coffee made the same way with half and half and two ice cubes, so we didn't have to wait to take that first sip. Our coffee was even better as we dunked Oreo cookies that we had taken apart to spread peanut butter on them. A few years later I started making fried peanut butter Oreos. Jeff called those a heart attack waiting to happen. Who could disagree? I surely couldn't because Jeff would have told you himself that he was never wrong. I so enjoyed those visits, and they continued even when my family had moved, and our home was no longer on Jeff's way home from work. Jeff enjoyed those visits, and he spent most of his time on my floor playing with my children.

As the years went by, my older boys participated in many different sports. The sporting events were also family events. Who would be there with us but my parents and my brother? Sometimes Jeff was the one clapping and cheering the loudest especially at the baseball games when one of his nephews would be pitching. We logged countless hours sitting on bleachers and lawn chairs watching the boys play ball. Jeff rarely missed a game. Jeff was so incredibly proud to be an uncle to those boys. My sons were so happy when Uncle Jeff was there to cheer them on.

Over the years, our family spent many days vacationing together on the Outer Banks of North Carolina. It was during those beach vacations that we made many wonderful memories that I still treasure today. In fact, I am writing this part of this book at our parents' home on the Outer Banks. For years, we would spend the month of July together at our parents' home. Jeff would be working on his driftwood beach shack creations, and I would be busy trying to get a better tan than Jeff. Yes another friendly competition between siblings'. Jeff and Mom loved working on their crafts together during our vacations. Jeff often depended on treasures from the beach to complete his beach shacks. Jeff would let me know when I needed to take the boys on a treasure hunt. The boys and I would take our beach wagon over that dune to start the treasure hunt. We would look for driftwood, sea fence, sea shells and any other treasures that washed up in the surf. Many times we had walked so far down the beach, dragging such a heavy load, we would have to call for a pick up because we had wandered a mile or two from the dune to our parents' house. Either Jeff or Dad would come to our rescue. The boys and I were amazed at how Jeff would take our beach finds and turn them into island artwork. The boys made sure every item that went into the wagon was something Uncle Jeff could use. Every time they picked something up the boys would say, "Hey Mom, can Uncle Jeff use this?" Time and time again I would have to say yes until this was an automatic response. Jeff loved emptying the wagon looking at the beach treasures we had collected. At times, we would have to laugh at some of the items that the boys put into the wagon. Let's just say some things could not be identified and others were obviously found on the beach because a dog owner did not clean up after their pet. I have many of Jeff's one of a kind pieces of art hanging on my walls of my family room. They are personalized, very special driftwood shacks that I will treasure forever.

I briefly mentioned that I liked to work on my tan whenever I could. I threw caution to the wind when it came to that perfect tan. Why did I do this year after year? You guessed it, another sibling competition. Jeff and I did not think about skin cancer risks; our only concern was who could get the darkest tan. Jeff could not be beat. My time on the beach was limited by having 3 young children, but Jeff and I always managed to find time to spend on the beach together. We would talk about anything and everything. Jeff was a planner so we often sat on the beach in July and talked about what to put on layaway for Christmas for the boys and our parents. I always made sure Jeff would be the one to do the shopping. Jeff was in tune with all of our Mom's collectables – me, well, not so much. Jeff had to teach me what to look for if I had to do any shopping. In the middle of the summer we even made a plan on how we were going to approach Black Friday. Jeff was a thinker, and that brain of his never seemed to stop planning. Oh, the things we planned while sitting on the beach!

The beach is where I feel the closest to my brother. Often when I am walking on the beach, I will write Jeff's name in the sand thinking that Jeff can see it from his place in Heaven. Sometimes it is hard to hold back the tears as

I watch the surf slowly wash Jeff's name in the sand. Just as cancer took away my brother, the ocean waves take away his name. I remember the countless hours that we would spend on the beach tanning, talking, throwing our cares to the wind and watching the waves crash to the shore. These are memories I treasure and will keep them tucked away into my heart. Jeff has been gone for close to five years as I write this and still there are times a memory will roll down my face in the form of a tear. Now, when I visit my parents' beach house, I choose to sleep in Jeff's room – the room our Mom has decorated with Jeff's art work and collections that he had in his home. I'm at peace there and wish my hectic schedule would allow for more days at the beach.

Something else my brother loved was a good campfire and cookout at our home in the country. My parents have a home, in Virginia, next to ours so getting together was very easy. Campfires, cooking hot dogs and hamburgers, and making s'mores are now among the memories that we treasure. I can visualize my brother sitting in the Adirondack chair that his oldest nephew, Trey, had made. One of my favorite pictures of Jeff is him sitting in that chair around the campfire. Now, when I'm having a rough day or really missing Jeff, I will often sit in that chair and feel comforted. Many memories were made and many stories were told around those campfires.

My brother passed away on my birthday in 2010. He was being cared for by my parents in their home. Many of our friends and family were gathered at my parents' home because Jeff had taken a turn for the worse. I promised Jeff that I would send him off to Heaven with one last campfire. As we waited for the funeral director to arrive, our friends and family made the biggest campfire that we ever had in that fire ring. The smoke was floating up to Heaven just as my brother had done minutes before. As Jeff's body was being carried down the outside stairs, I asked the funeral home staff to stop and uncover my brother's face so he could see that I had indeed kept my promise.

I needed a bit of inspiration to figure out where to go next with my portion on this book, so I headed to the rooftop deck of the beach house. I could visualize my brother standing on the corner of the deck waiting for the perfect wind gust, so he could launch his shark kite. He loved flying his shark kite. I, on the other hand, had a pirate kite. You may be thinking a shark kite and a pirate kite? These particular kites had significant meaning to us. Jeff and I were die hard Parrotheads, trying to live life or imagine life as Jimmy Buffett wrote about in his songs. Parrotheads were said to be sharks that lived on the land. Parrotheads embraced the adventurous lives of those pirates who sailed the waters so long ago. The song "Fins" referred to those sharks who lived on the land. The song "A Pirate Looks at 40" referred to Jimmy Buffett and Parrotheads arriving 200 years too late. I am not advocating for or against pirates; however, these are two songs that are favorites among Parrotheads. It was not until I returned from living in Florida, and Jeff returned from college after his first go round with cancer, that we realized, without knowing, that each of us had developed the love of Jimmy Buffett music and could call ourselves Parrotheads. Jeff faded away from his earthly life with Jimmy Buffett music playing softly in the background. I know Jeff would not have wanted to leave this earth in any other way.

Year after year Jeff and I would plan our attack on scoring Jimmy Buffett tickets and set out for the greatest tailgate party of the year. If you have never been to a Buffett tailgating party, I am here to tell you that a gravel parking lot quickly becomes transformed into a Buffett paradise with the most creative beach and pirate decorations. Jeff and I were able to step up in the tailgating world when my husband and I purchased our first motorhome. Jeff and I named that motorhome "The Parrotdise". We decorated the RV and turned it in to a tropical paradise. We had graduated to the big leagues and there was no turning back. So many people would comment on our decorations. Jeff was creative and knew how to decorate for any event. Being Parrotheads was a big part of who we were as adults. We made sure that my oldest two sons were Parrotheads too. We had my oldest son flipping cheeseburgers for us at the concert when he was just five years old. Once you made it through kindergarten then you were old enough to go see Jimmy Buffett. Jeff's last Buffett concert was in 2009. I hoped and prayed that Jeff would be well enough to go to the Buffett concert in 2010. The concert was Labor Day weekend and Jeff was not up to going to the concert. Jeff insisted that I go to the concert so Mom and I went together fighting back tears knowing Jeff was at home. Jeff did listen to the concert on his computer and somehow knowing that made it easier for us to enjoy part of the show. However, there was no tailgating for us that year. We simply went because Jeff wanted us to go.

Jeff had transformed his backyard into a tropical paradise. We didn't care if the palm trees were electric. Those tiki torches lit up the yard, and we would sit out in the yard and watch his pug, Buddy, run around until he was tired and finally would settle down and lay beside his master. I actually think Buddy was the master, but who am I to say? Jeff and I treasured our time together in his yard, and that is where we would talk about almost anything. Many times we would have company sitting in the backyard. Jeff's friends became my friends, and some of my friends became Jeff's friends. You never knew who would show up on any given night, but that electrical tropical paradise was never more than a match stick or a light switch away.

About two weeks before my birthday, Jeff insisted that my Mom go to the garage and find the box that contained the birthday presents he had bought for me. My brother was insistent that these gifts be found. No easy task because all of Jeff's belongings were packed and stored in my parents' garage. But never the less, my Mom did find the box. At 9:45pm on September 23rd, 2010 my Mom asked me if I wanted my birthday presents from my brother. She told me that they were going to make me cry, but by this point in the day, I did not care. I wanted to cry; I wanted my presents. Jeff knew I collected Tom Clark figurines, and he found one for me - "Florence', a nurse. I also collect carousel horses and snow globes. Jeff had found a snow globe carousel horse, and when wound, it played "Happy Birthday". I wound the snow globe again, so it would continue to play "Happy Birthday". I wasn't very far from where Jeff laid, unresponsive, as he had been all day. Dad and Gram called us to come into the bedroom because my brother's respirations had changed. I went to check on my brother, and my Mom came in to his room carrying the carousel music box still playing "Happy Birthday". Mom said, "Look Jeff, we gave Kim her birthday presents." Within seconds after "Happy Birthday" stopped playing, my brother took his last breath. Mom said she believed that Jeff was waiting for them to give me my gifts. When he knew I had his gifts, his last wish had been fulfilled, and he was ready to go home to God. I am a nurse, and I knew Hospice would need the time of death. I laid my head over my brother's heart and waited for that final heartbeat. God had called my brother home. No more cancer; no more pain, and no more worry about test results. The only thing left to do was grieve and keep my brother's spirit alive.

Healing has been a long process, and five years later, there is not a day that goes by that I don't think of my brother multiple times a day. I watch for signs; I look for Angel pennies; I look at his pictures, and I listen to our favorite music. The hurt doesn't go away, but eventually, you do find a new normal in your life.

I was not a very spiritual person when we lost Jeff. I was lost and broken. I took a trip to Florida in August of 2011. I planned to go to Jacksonville Beach to visit friends. I knew my cousin, Lonnie McDaniel, lived in Jacksonville, and I knew he was a pastor. I connected with my cousin on Facebook only weeks earlier. I had only met Lonnie once in my life. Would he see my message? Would he help me to understand about death? Would he even respond to my message? The answer to these questions was 'yes." Lonnie responded within hours of me sending the message. I spent many hours with my cousin and his family for the next week. It was in Florida where I bought a version of the Bible that I could understand. I asked Lonnie where I should start, and he said, "The Book of John." Looking back I know why he told me to read that book first. He wanted me to understand baptism and the significance of this event. Although I had been baptized as an infant, on August 7th, 2011, I chose to have my cousin baptize me again. My spiritual journey began at St. Mary's River in Hilliard, Florida and enabled me to be able to deal with my grief. This was the first time that I realized that my brother was living an eternal life. It was then I knew that September 23rd, 2010 at 9:58 p.m., was not goodbye, it was I'll see you later.

I miss him more everyday but I treasure every memory and all the time that we had together. It was September 23rd, 2010 when Jeff became that "Pirate who Left at 40". That night, I put my two hands together like "Fins" above my head in Parrothead style and I believe that Jeff could see my peculiar "fins to the left, fins to the right" wave to the Heavens.

CHAPTER 13

JEFF'S STORY

To completely understand Jeff's story, I feel it was important to give you a glimpse of his life journey. As an infant and a toddler, Jeff had many of the normal childhood illnesses - colds, sore throats, and ear infections. These eventually led to his first surgery, a tonsillectomy, at the age of three. His bright, sparkling eyes, and a smile that wouldn't stop, captured the hearts of his nurses from the moment they met him. Jeff amazed his doctors and nurses with, what they called, his determination. At that time, I just called it stubbornness. Just a few hours after his tonsillectomy, that boy was eating pretzels! Did he want the cool, soothing popsicles they typically offered after a tonsillectomy back in the 70's? Not Jeff! He was determined to have pretzels – and he did!

Jeff's first admission to the hospital and having surgery was just a mere annoyance to this child. There was no keeping him down, and nothing was going to interfere with his playtime! With the surgery behind him, he was ready to take on the role of a very active, energetic toddler and preschooler. Jeff's childhood, teen, and college years were routine. They included the activities of every other normal kid. Jeff did all the typical boy things during his elementary and middle school years. He participated in the school patrol program, boy scouts, and baseball teams. Jeff also enjoyed our many family camping and beach vacations.

Journalism captured Jeff's attention when he got to Gar-Field High School. Soon he was a reporter for the Hyphen, his high school newspaper.

He wrote many informative and interesting stories during his high school years. In college he majored in Business Administration and minored in Psychology. He worked hard to obtain his degree but still had time for fun in his free time. He enjoyed being in a dart league, and of course, all those parties that college kids seem to find time for. Jeff's very normal, routine life changed on the day he finished his last college exam, just one week before his college graduation.

Jeff's first bout with cancer was in 1992 when he was a student at Elon College in Burlington, NC. The day was May 16th, 1992. It was mid-afternoon when he called to tell me he had just finished his last college exam and had a week to go before graduation. Jeff was a dedicated student who studied and worked hard through his four years of college. Now it was time to relax, time to party, and time to have fun before graduation day. Jeff told me the first party was that night – and then said, "Don't worry Mom, it's at our place, so there won't be any drinking and driving." The next call I got was from Jeff's roommate, Steve, at 1:00 a.m. on May 17, 1992. Steve's words to me when I answered the phone were, "Mrs. Crislip, Jeff is okay, but he is in the hospital." That didn't sound at all okay to me - and as it turned out, it wasn't.

Everyone at the party was having a great time, but as it got a bit warm inside, they decided to continue the party outside around the lake. One of Jeff's friends - all in fun - picked him up and threw him over his shoulder. Jeff didn't land on his feet, but was very proud that he didn't spill his can of beer on the way down. His earlier laughter quickly turned to pain as he landed on the concrete floor of the gazebo. One of Jeff's friends dialed 911. The rescue squad arrived and took him to Burlington Hospital. There x-rays were taken to reveal, not only a broken femur, but also a tumor in his leg. One had nothing to do with the other, but breaking his leg most likely saved his life. Jeff was transferred to Duke University Medical Center where he remained for the next twenty nine days. Jeff's Dad and I threw a few things in a suitcase and were on our way to the hospital within thirty minutes of receiving the call. What we didn't know then was that we wouldn't be coming back home until Jeff was released from the hospital in the middle of June. His case was complicated - they couldn't use a pin in his femur to set the break because the pin would have gone into the tumor. Jeff was in traction for two weeks while they tried to determine if the tumor was malignant.

During those two weeks in the hospital, Jeff had a needle biopsy, a surgical biopsy, and every other test and scan that was available. The doctors still didn't have a firm diagnosis. His records and slides that had been done in the lab at Duke were sent to the Armed Forces Institute of Pathology (AFIP) in Washington, DC. The AFIP deals only with tumors, but they were not successful in coming up with a diagnosis for Jeff's tumor. At that point, Jeff's doctor made the decision to set his leg in a full leg cast and send him home to let the broken femur heal. All the while, tests and research continued to search for and find a diagnosis. At that point everything concerning Jeff's case and the tumor was sent to Metafiore Hospital in New York City. Here a diagnosis was finally made. Finally, there was a doctor who had seen this type of tumor, and in fact, had written a book about it. It was then that we heard the words we didn't want to hear. It was a malignant tumor - Hemangioendothelioma (he-man-gee-o-end-o-th-e-lee-o-ma). If I started telling you about that type of tumor, you would put this book down in a heartbeat, so I won't go there.

The treatment was high doses of radiation – mega doses of radiation. However, because radiation stops growth, the broken femur had to be completely healed before the radiation treatments could begin. When the diagnosis was finally made, it was the end of June and Jeff was in the full leg cast waiting for the break to heal. It was September before the broken femur had healed and the cast removed. Jeff started his radiation treatments the day after Labor Day - September, 1992. The treatments continued – five days a week until the day before Thanksgiving - November, 1992. He did great with the treatments until the last three weeks when he started having some nausea and redness to his leg that was similar to a sun burn. All things considered, Jeff did fine during the time it took to heal the broken femur and with the radiation treatments. We continued to make the four hour trek back and forth to Duke University Medical Center for six years. In the beginning it was every two months, the second year was every three months, the third year was every four months.

Going to Duke for those appointments was always interesting when it came to locating Jeff's medical records. Because Jeff's cancer was very rare, his doctors requested permission from Jeff to use his case for teaching in the classrooms at Duke University School of Medicine. It didn't surprise me at all when Jeff gave his permission, making it possible for others to learn from his experience and, hopefully, gain more knowledge of this type of cancer. It was three years after the radiation treatments before the doctor told us that the tumor was completely gone. Those words were like music to our ears. We knew it was shrinking, but it wasn't completely gone for three years. Years three through six Jeff and I traveled to Duke every six months. Finally, after six years in remission, Jeff's doctors gave him a clean bill of health.

Jeff was cancer free for fourteen years. He was the picture of good health - energetic, working out at the gym, a slim, trim, and buff young man. The week before Christmas in 2005, Jeff noticed a very small lump under his arm. He thought he had most likely strained his muscles at the gym while he was lifting weights. He had been planning a trip to Florida to visit friends to ring in the New Year. He decided to take the trip and said if the lump didn't go away, he would go to the doctor as soon as he got back. Not only did the lump not go away, it doubled in size. Needless to say, off to the doctor he went. He had no symptoms except for the lump under his arm. He had lost some weight, but he was trying to drop a few pounds, so he really didn't think anything about the weight loss at that time. The doctor told Jeff to come back in two weeks since he had no other symptoms. Three days after his first appointment, Jeff started having night sweats so he immediately went back to see the doctor. The doctor made arrangements for Jeff to see a surgeon the very next day. The surgeon admitted Jeff to the hospital the following day to have the lump removed. So now, once again, we waited for results. A few days later, Jeff was diagnosed with Non-Hodgkin's Lymphoma, Stage IV, the most serious stage. We knew that another journey down a very long road was ahead. That journey began in February of 2006 when Jeff started chemotherapy treatments.

Because of the advanced stage of the cancer, Dr. Charles Maurer, Jeff's doctor in Fredericksburg, VA, was conferring with Dr. Brent Perkins at MCV/VCU in Richmond, VA. MCV is a teaching hospital which meant they had chemotherapy drugs there that weren't available locally. Both doctors were in agreement; Jeff would have all his treatments at MCV. The chemotherapy drugs would be wicked and, of course, had the potential to cause some nasty side effects. Because one of the chemotherapy drugs (high dose Methotrexate) was so intense, Jeff needed his treatments done as an inpatient. Due to the toxic effects of high dose Methotrexate, certain precautions were necessary and Jeff had to be monitored after it was given. Six hours after the Methotrexate finished, the rescue drug, Lucavoran was started along with extra fluids. At that point, Jeff had to be monitored to check the level of Methotrexate in his body. His Methotrexate level needed to be .05 within 72 hours. If the Methotrexate level wasn't falling fast enough, the Lucavoran and fluids were increased.

From February through the end of June, Jeff and I spent one week in the hospital for his treatments followed by two weeks at home. The two weeks spent at home was to give his blood counts a chance to rebound before the next treatment. I stayed at the hospital, in the room with Jeff, each time he was admitted for treatments. Jeff wanted me to stay with him and there was no way I was leaving him there to go through his treatments alone. The first six or seven days of our ten days at home were difficult days. We quickly learned how to be very proactive with the nausea and pain medications. Jeff usually felt pretty good at the end of the ten days when it was time to be admitted again. We made the most of those hospital days – we talked, played on our computers, walked the halls together, took naps, and watched TV. As I mentioned in the caregiver chapter, I valued every day and the time we spent together. We realized that life as you know it can change in a heartbeat and you need to make the most of every single day you have on this earth.

Because of germs, Jeff had to be careful about being around people. While his blood counts were low, which was caused by the chemotherapy, this was something we obsessed about. This was especially true in public places. Fortunately, he was able to make it through all his treatments without getting any infections. He had his last chemotherapy treatment in mid-June of 2006. At this point, getting blood drawn, having scans and tests became routine. Four weeks after Jeff completed his treatments, he had a lumbar puncture to check his spinal fluid. Once again we received news we didn't want to hear and weren't prepared for - cancer cells showed up in his spinal fluid – not many, but definitely cancer cells. I remember Jeff dropping his head to digest the bad news. My heart was pounding, and I felt like I was going to drop to the floor. After what seemed to be an eternity, but in reality was less than a minute, Jeff broke the silence in the room. He looked up and said – "That means I have to work harder to beat this – what's next doc?" In my opinion, that was an amazing reaction to the news he had been given. The next step was radiation to the central nervous system. Preparations were made; the radiation plan was developed and it was determined that Jeff would have a total of thirteen treatments - eleven to his spine and, because the cancer cells could travel to his brain, through the central nervous system, he would have two radiation treatments to his brain. It was then that the doctors told Jeff that because he was young, and otherwise healthy, he would be a prime candidate for a stem cell transplant.

To qualify for a stem cell transplant, you must have healthy, strong organs, and be certain you have no infections of any type. For the next two months, Jeff and I spent lots of time going to doctors and specialists having all his organs tested to make sure every single part of his body was in tip top shape. He also had to go to the dentist to be sure his teeth were infection free. Jeff passed every test with flying colors, except one. After a visit to the dentist, he had to have his wisdom teeth pulled. The teeth were starting to abscess, which, as you know, is infection. Our next trip was to an oral surgeon, so Jeff could have all four wisdom teeth extracted at the same time. To be certain the infection would be totally gone, Jeff was on antibiotics for two weeks after the surgery. Finally, the preparation for the transplant was completed.

The next step is a big one - harvesting the stem cells. Since Jeff had taken all the chemotherapy and thirteen radiation treatments, Dr. Perkins, Jeff's Oncologist, and Dr. Song, his Radiation Oncologist, felt there would be less risk of rejection if he used his own stem cells. This procedure is called an autogulous stem cell transplant. The risk of transplanting a cancer cell was less than the risk of rejection if they would use donated stem cells for the transplant. The stem cell harvesting process is totally amazing. As Jeff sat down in a huge, comfy recliner, with a technician by his side, he was covered with soft, warm blankets. He had an IV inserted into one arm taking the blood out of his body into a harvesting machine. This miraculous little machine then separated the stem cells from the other parts of the blood. As Jeff's blood spun around in this machine, that might I add resembled the inside of a washing machine, the stem cells were released into a container. The rest of the blood was then pumped back into his body through an IV that had been inserted into his other arm. They needed to harvest four million stem cells for the transplant. It took two visits and a total of seven hours to harvest the four million stem cells. With the harvesting successful and complete, Jeff's stem cells would be frozen until the big day.

Jeff was admitted to MCV Hospital at the end of September of 2006, and the process of preparing him for the transplant continued. The first three days he had massive, high dose chemotherapy. On days four and five, Jeff had total body radiation. Day number six was a day of rest. On the seventh day, October 3rd, 2006, Jeff had his stem cell transplant. After the transplant, one of Jeff's nurses told him that October 3rd was his new birthday!! From that point on, we celebrated two birthdays – July 23, the day he was born, and October 3, his new birthday. The transplant was done in his room through his IV as I sat and watched the entire process. It was incredible to watch those little cells going into his body. What an amazing experience to watch new life going into my son's body giving him an opportunity for a new lease on life. Jeff looked at his Dad and me several times during the transplant and we all smiled. So now, we had to learn a whole new way of life as those little stem cells start to grow, and Jeff's counts start to go back to normal levels.

The first week after the transplant was pretty rough for Jeff. He basically had no immune system, no strength, no energy, frequent nausea, and just wanted to sleep. He slept most of the day and most of the night for the first few days, but the doctors only let him get away with that for a few days – they wanted him to get up and get moving. It was so hard for him at first because he was so weak and had no stamina at all. Day by day, he began to improve and after about a week, that determination to win the fight was back full force. He wanted out of that place!!! It didn't matter that we decorated his room beautifully, Margarittaville style - he still wanted OUT of that hospital

The nurses loved coming to Jeff's room - they said it was like going to a tropical island for a mini vacation. His room was decorated from top to bottom with beachy, Jimmy Buffett, tropical things, complete with a little lighted palm tree. We also hung every card that Jeff got on the bulletin board, which filled up very fast, so I started hanging them on the walls. Everyone loved Jeff's room - and they loved taking care of Jeff. The nurses always told me that he was the most pleasant patient they ever had- always smiling, always a positive attitude, and they loved his sarcastic side. We had to laugh when they told us that the nurses fought over who was going to get to be Jeff's nurse and decided to take turns.

Holding On While Letting Go

Another idea the nurses liked was Jeff's theory about the proper attire to wear in the hospital. Jeff always said – "If you dress like you're sick, you will feel sick." There would be no hospital gowns or PJ's for him. Jeff was a hoot - he wore cargo shorts, Jimmy Buffett t-shirts, flip flops and a baseball cap. You never saw Jeff walking the halls unless he was completely dressed. Funny thing - there was a young lady - probably about Jeff's age that apparently had the same idea. She was always dressed in lounging pants, a pretty shirt, and matching scarf for her head – and, she always had on her makeup. She and Jeff were the only ones who looked like they were ready to go out and have some fun - everyone else had on their gowns or PJ's and, as Jeff put it, looked sick. As a spectator, I had to agree – Jeff and this young lady, dressed in their survivor outfits and smiling as they walked the halls, looked great. On the other hand, the patients wearing their hospital gowns or PJ's looked sad and sick. Jeff and this pretty, young gal, both in their survivor attire smiled and looked up as they walked the halls. The PJ and gown people just walked along, most looking down and rarely did you see them smile. Again, I must agree with Jeff – "If you dress like you're sick, you will feel and act like you're sick."

Knowing he had to regain his strength and muster up some energy before he could be discharged from the hospital, Jeff did his best to eat as much as he possibly could, even though he had no appetite. He was up and out of that bed every day and walked laps around the oncology floor at least three times a day, and most days, more. We knew in advance that Jeff would not be allowed to go home when he was discharged from the hospital. It was mandatory that he be within twenty minutes of the hospital, at all times, until his blood counts rebounded to a certain level. We lived in Fredericksburg, VA which is an hour away from the hospital. We had a couple of options - rent an apartment, stay at the Hospitality House provided by MCV which was adjacent to the hospital, or convince the team of doctors to let him stay in our motor home at a campground that was fifteen minutes away. Jeff's doctors were hesitant about the motor home at first because of the molds and germs that could be in a campground and could be a danger to Jeff's immune system. My argument was that an apartment would have more germs than our motor home because of other people having lived in it, not to mention that it would cost a small fortune for a short term lease. The Hospitality House would be full of germs as well – each patient had his/her own room, but everyone shared the same kitchen to prepare meals. There would be many other patients and caregivers there too - meaning even more germs. Our motor home was new and had only been used twice by my husband and me. Jeff and I told them we would stay inside the motor home except for our daily trips to the clinic for lab work. They finally told us we could stay in the motor home at the campground but they wanted us to take some extra precautions. They wanted the motor home to have a HEPA air filtration system and a water filter. We had no problem at all with getting the equipment they requested to be sure that Jeff would be as safe as possible.

Cris and I cleaned the trailer and took it to the campground just before Jeff went into the hospital to start the stem cell transplant process. I was not happy when I found out that no one was allowed to spend the night on the transplant floor, but I had no choice but to comply. This was the first time I had not been able to stay with Jeff when he was in the hospital. Every night after Jeff's transplant, I went to the motor home to shower and sleep. I got up early every morning and went back to the hospital to be with Jeff. This was my routine until Jeff was discharged. Jeff was released nineteen days after the transplant which was just about record time for discharge after a stem cell transplant.

We left the hospital and drove to the campground and the motor home which we called home for another four weeks. We made daily trips to the clinic, which often took several hours, because of waiting on the lab results. Depending on the results, there were days when Jeff needed to have an infusion of blood or platelets which meant spending almost the entire day at the clinic. Jeff was still very weak, and his immune system was still almost non-existent, so the days when our clinic visits took many hours were not easy for him. He got though those visits without complaining, but always threw in a few sarcastic remarks while he was there. His remarks often brought smiles to the other patients in the waiting room.

Life after a stem cell transplant is truly a learning experience. Those of us with a normal immune system never give a second thought to the routine things in life that could be life threatening to a cancer patient who has received a stem cell transplant. During the transplant process, the chemotherapy and total body radiation kills all the adult stem cells in your body which means your immune system is non-existent. After the transplant, the new stem cells are babies - so to speak. While the stem cells are growing to maturity, which can take up to five years, extra precautions need to be taken in an effort to avoid germs and infections. As Jeff's caregiver, I was given many instructions by the oncologist and the oncology nurses, and also a book to read that gave me even more advice on the proper way to care for my son in this new phase of his life. Some of the things we had to do religiously were: always use disposable plates, cups, and plastic utensils, and drink purified bottled water - the water filter that we had to install in the motor home was to prevent germs from getting on Jeff's skin when he took a shower. Jeff could not have fresh raw vegetables, and fresh fruit had to be washed thoroughly and peeled before he could eat them. There was one trick I had to learn that presented a challenge for me - I had to peel the fruit without touching the fruit itself —now that took some practice, but I must say I mastered that art in a very short period of time. Jeff and I decided that we should have taken out stock in Clorox wipes and Purell hand sanitizer - we used both like they grew on trees and were free for the taking. I did everything I could think of to keep Jeff safe and his atmosphere germ free.

Because of the constant threat of infection as the stem cells began to mature, I had to take Jeff's temperature several times a day. If his temperature went to 100.5 - that was a sign of an infection, and we had to go to the hospital immediately. This was the main reason we had to stay no more than twenty minutes away from the hospital. Fortunately, all the precautions we used worked - Jeff never got a fever – a special thank you to the makers of Clorox wipes and Purell hand sanitizer. When we returned to our campground home after our daily visits to the clinic, the first thing we did was take a nice long nap. These days were exhausting for me, so I could only begin to imagine the exhaustion Jeff was feeling. Jeff and I spent many hours watching movies – something that didn't require using much energy. Jeff's dad was not retired at that time, but he would come to stay with us on the weekends – something we both looked forward to.

Those were challenging times and a real learning experience for sure, but we made it through without any complications whatsoever. Finally, the day came in the middle of November when Jeff's lab work showed his counts were continuing to go up, and because he had been infection free since the transplant, we were given the green light to go home. Although it was a bit scary for me, leaving my comfort zone of being close to the hospital and Jeff's Oncologist, it was wonderful to see Jeff so excited about going home. I put my fears and insecurities in my pocket, and home we went.

It was wonderful to be home for Thanksgiving Day, and we had so very much to be thankful for. Being home was great but also presented a new set of challenges. Jeff's stem cells were babies so it was very important that we continue to be diligent about trying to keep germs out of our world. It takes up to five years for stem cells to completely mature, so we needed to be sure the germ patrol was on duty at all times. We were given more reading material to help us "think like a germ" and become familiar

Holding On While Letting Go

with their hiding places. I'm sure you've seen how the grocery stores now have the sanitizing wipes to clean the handles on the carts between users. That's great, but there are so many other places that you normally don't think about that are also germ laden. Menus in restaurants are one of the worst - just think of how many people touch those menus and then wonder what they touch before picking up that menu. If you go to a restaurant that offers a buffet, you won't necessarily be touching a menu, but did you ever think about how many germs are on the handles of the serving spoons at a buffet or salad bar? Purell hand sanitizer was one of the best tools we had for keeping the germs at bay when eating out, always using it after finishing with the menu and after each trip to a buffet or salad bar. Germs are on every single thing we touch or come in contact with, such as door knobs, light switch covers, TV remotes, cells phones, toilet handles, the handle on the dog's leash, the steering wheel in your car, gas pumps, your wallet, money, and the list goes on - including our computer key boards and that little mouse!!! Clorox wipes took care of the germs on those items and many others.

Even though Jeff's stem cells were no longer babies, as they moved towards adolescence, Jeff still had to be careful about some of the things he ate. For example - no soft ice cream – if the machines were not being cleaned properly they would harbor germs. Fresh vegetables were off limits because of the pesticides that were used while they were being grown. If Jeff ate meat, it had to be well done. Fresh fruits had to be washed - even bananas. How many people wash a banana before they peel it? Think about it - when you have bananas in your home and all at once the fruit flies appear – where do they come from? Oh yes, I am going to tell you where those fruit flies come from – those invisible little fruit fly eggs that are on the banana skins. So, if you don't wash that banana before you peel it, where do those fruit fly eggs go? I'll leave that question for you to figure out. Trust me, to this day, I wash my bananas before I peel them, and I always will.

Jeff started feeling much better, was getting stronger, and had more energy with every day that passed. Not long after we got home, and as soon as his counts were high enough, he was ready to get out and about. He still had to be mindful of being around crowds of people where he would be exposed to germs from others coughing, sneezing, etc. He was getting stronger every day but still very susceptible to infections, so we were very observant of people when we were out in public and always had our defense weapons, Clorox wipes and Purell hand sanitizer, with us at all times. If we went out to the craft stores or to a mall, we went at times when we felt the stores would be less busy – during the day when most people were working. We tried to stay off to ourselves as much as we could when we were out in public while those little stem cells continued to grow. There were many challenges along the way, but we learned to accept them, did the best we could to stay healthy, and went on with our life.

Jeff and I continued our scheduled visits to the Massey Cancer Center and Dalton Oncology Clinic in Richmond for lab work and appointments with his Oncologist. Jeff had an appointment just before Christmas and was given an awesome gift – a piece of paper from the lab, with the results of his blood work, was in the doctor's hands. Dr. Perkins handed that paper to Jeff so he could not only hear, but see for himself that his counts were excellent. Jeff then heard the words he had been waiting to hear for nearly a year – "You can go back to work." Needless to say, we were very thankful that our prayers had been answered in the way that we prayed they would be – Jeff was healthy enough to return to his normal life – still taking precautions of course. We had everything we wanted to make our Christmas holiday perfect.

Jeff was a security specialist for Prince William County Schools and worked at Beville Middle School in Dale City, Virginia. He was part of the administrative team and worked not only doing all the crisis planning, making sure the building was safe and secure, but also worked with the students trying to help those who needed a little push to stay on the right track. Jeff's minor in Psychology helped him in knowing how to deal with the students and how to earn their trust, I'm sure. Jeff was so happy to be back at work and get back to a normal life after an entire year of hospitals and treatments in 2006. The first year after the transplant was a year of taking precautions to stay healthy and adjusting to working while not being quite back to normal in the energy department.

The next two years went great for Jeff. He had more energy, so the work days were easier; he went back to working out although, because of the "germ factor" at the gym, he worked out at home. He was able to travel and spend many weeks at our beach house in North Carolina and visiting friends in Georgia and Florida. Jeff went for scans every three months, and everything continued to be fine - even his last scan early in November of 2009 was clear.

It was December of 2009 when Jeff first started thinking something wasn't right. He was worried about his memory because he would forget things frequently - but chocked some of it up to heading towards being 40 years old. He had no symptoms, and with all of his scans and tests being normal, he thought maybe he was just being a little paranoid. On December 19th, we had a major snow storm in Fredericksburg, Virginia – two feet of the white stuff covered the ground.

Jeff lived in a townhouse development and was outside shoveling snow with his neighbors. One special neighbor - Sandy, who was like a Mom to Jeff, kept on shoveling long after most everyone else had stopped for the day. Jeff called me and told me he and his neighbors had been shoveling for several hours. He told me he was tired, but he wasn't going to stop shoveling until Sandy did. I reminded Jeff that he shouldn't wear himself out and take a chance on getting sick. He said, "Mom, she's 60 years old. I'm not letting her stay out there shoveling by herself." That's the way Jeff was - always helping someone when he could. Jeff and Sandy shoveled that heavy snow for a total of six hours. Of course Jeff was exhausted, but otherwise felt good. He loved snow, and he and Sandy had a great time. I believe the snowstorm, that day when two feet of snow fell to the ground, was a blessing in disguise.

The next day, December 20, 2010, Jeff's legs and arms were weak - to be expected after shoveling snow for six hours. Two days later – three days before Christmas - Jeff started having mild tremors in his arm. The day before Christmas, he started to have tremors in his leg. On Christmas Day, he had more tremors a couple of times. They weren't anything major, just a little shakiness for less than a minute and then it would stop. Of course there are no doctors available on Christmas Day, but Jeff had already decided that he would call to make an appointment with his oncologist first thing in January when the world went back to work. He had the tremors off and on during the week after Christmas – still not bad tremors, but there were a couple that lasted longer than a minute. Of course we were all very concerned and I'm sure Jeff was more concerned than he let us know.

Jeff went to work on January 4, 2010 but wasn't feeling well. He called me to let me know that he was going to call Dr. Perkins to get an appointment because he was certain something wasn't right. That morning, Jeff told his principal and his assistant principal that he hadn't been feeling well for a couple weeks and that he was going to call and make an appointment with his oncologist. He told them he just wanted them to know he wasn't feeling well just in case he had to leave school early. After that conversation, Jeff went on about his normal day until 1:50 p.m. For Jeff and for us, most of the next two hours would remain a mystery.

Everyone was busy as they went through the hectic school day and didn't notice that Jeff hadn't been around for a while. But that wasn't anything unusual if he was busy with a child in his office. Jeff was almost always outside when the buses arrived, so he could supervise the students as they got on the buses. As the buses began to leave the parking lot, the assistant principal noticed that Jeff wasn't out at the buses like he usually was, but didn't think too much of it, thinking he was still dealing with an issue with a child, or possibly a parent. Again, everyone went on with their daily routine.

What no one knew was that Jeff had collapsed in his office. He had a major seizure and was totally paralyzed on his right side. Jeff went in and out of consciousness as he struggled to drag himself across the floor of his office to get to the door - which was locked. Jeff regularly kept his door locked when dealing with students, so they would be able to speak to him confidentially. Thank goodness handicapped handles had been installed on all the doors throughout the school in July of 2009. Jeff would never have been able to open the door with a regular door knob so who knows when he would have been found. It was 3:45 p.m. when he managed to drag himself to the door. He stretched to grab onto the handle to unlatch the door to open it and dragged himself into the doorway, so he could be seen. As he laid in the doorway, completely paralyzed on his right side, he was able to hear what was going on but unable to speak or make a sound; he waited to be found. A teacher found him, immediately called the nurse, and dialed 911 for the rescue squad. Later, Jeff told me that each time he would wake up, all he could think of was that the door was locked, and if he didn't make it to the door before everyone left for the day, he would lay there and die. Even now, my heart is pounding just writing about what he had to endure. When he collapsed, he also hit his head on something in his office and was bleeding. He knew he was bleeding because he could feel the wetness, knowing he was paralyzed on his right side, and he couldn't speak - he was terrified as he struggled to drag himself to the door fearing that he wouldn't be found before his colleagues went home.

It was nearly four o'clock when I received the call from the school secretary to let me know that something had happened to Jeff, and he was going to be transported to the hospital. She connected me to the phone in

Jeff's office, so I could speak to the rescue chief. I begged him to let me speak to Jeff, was told that Jeff couldn't speak, and they thought he could possibly have had a stroke. I was scared beyond belief when they told me Jeff couldn't speak. The rescue chief was talking to me on a speaker phone when I asked if Jeff could hear me. I'm not sure how he knew, but he told me that Jeff was aware of what was going on. Tears filled my eyes and my heart started racing and to make it even worse, Cris and I were in Pennsylvania visiting my mother. Needless to say, we left immediately and raced down the highway to the hospital. Normally this would be a five and a half hour trip; however, we arrived at the hospital in four hours. A couple of days later, Jeff told me he did hear everything I said, and he knew we were going to get to the hospital as fast as we could.

Jeff was being transported to Potomac Hospital in Woodbridge, VA. I immediately called my best friend, Robin Simler, who lives in Woodbridge, to ask her to go to the hospital to be with Jeff until his sister, Kim, could get there. Robin happened to be on her way home from shopping and was sitting at the traffic light at the intersection at Potomac Hospital when I reached her. She turned into the hospital parking lot and waited for the ambulance to arrive. I was very relieved to know she was there waiting on Jeff. Jeff told me later when he knew Robin was there, he felt better. I then called his sister, and she went immediately to the hospital too, but was 35 minutes away. Jeff arrived at the hospital in the ambulance with ten of his friends from school following in their own vehicles. He was able to speak a couple words by then, which I was relieved to hear. I stayed on the phone with friends who were waiting at the hospital almost the entire drive back to Virginia.

Shortly after Jeff arrived at the hospital, he had another seizure; this time it was a mild one. Thankfully, he wasn't alone; Kim was with him when he had that seizure. He was still paralyzed on his right side from the seizure he had in his office. He had started to regain his speech, but again, lost the ability to speak after the second seizure, but only for a few minutes.

Holding On While Letting Go

Jeff had an MRI immediately which confirmed there was a tumor in his brain. At that point, Kim was told that Jeff was going to be transferred to Fairfax Inova Trauma Center by Life Flight. My heart was pounding, and the tears were flowing as I continued to be updated on everything that was happening with my son while I was still hours away. Our oldest grandson, Trey, was also at Potomac Hospital with Jeff, so when they were told that Jeff was being flown to Fairfax, Trey left immediately, so he would be at the hospital waiting for Jeff when the helicopter landed. Kim stayed with Jeff at the first hospital until the helicopter was in flight. Kim and all of Jeff's co-workers were on their way to Fairfax Trauma Center as soon as the helicopter left the ground. Even though I knew Jeff wasn't alone, and I was being updated by cell phone every step of the way, my heart was breaking knowing I wasn't there for my son.

Knowing when Jeff was able to speak, there would be two things he would ask about: his dog, Buddy, and his car. Robin and the assistant principal from Jeff's school went to Jeff's townhouse to get Buddy. They took Buddy to Robin's house and then went to the school to get Jeff's car which they also took to Robin's house before going back to the hospital to be with Jeff.

Jeff arrived at Fairfax hospital at 7:30 p.m. and was taken to the ER where he had another mild seizure. Fortunately, he was able to speak through that one and had also started to regain some movement in his arm. The trauma team went into action immediately, and by the time Cris and I arrived at the hospital, a neurosurgeon was waiting to talk to us. It was then that we heard the words we feared the most – they thought most likely the tumor meant that the Non-Hodgkin's Lymphoma had reared its ugly head once again. The next several hours were like a nightmare, and of course I was convinced that these doctors didn't know what they were talking about. I was desperate to get Jeff transferred to the Medical College of Virginia Hospital (MCV) in Richmond and back to the doctors he had been seeing for the past three years. By noon the next day, I had reached

Jeff's oncologist at MCV and at 10:00 p.m. that night, Jeff was transported by ambulance to MCV in Richmond.

We arrived in Richmond at midnight with a team of doctors waiting on Jeff. Things happened fast at that point - another MRI and a CT scan were first on the agenda and they quickly started him on seizure medication by IV. Early the morning of January 6th, we heard the same words we had heard at Fairfax – the tumor was most likely Non-Hodgkin's Lymphoma. The only way to be sure it was the Lymphoma was to do a biopsy. The paralysis had begun to go away, so after Jeff's oncologist thought the anti-seizure medication was working and Jeff was stable, he felt he could go home for the weekend. He wanted Jeff to rest and get some strength back while preparations were made for him to have brain surgery the following week to do the biopsy. I was frightened beyond belief at the thought of taking him home, but of course Jeff wanted to go, and so we did.

We went home on Friday - everything seemed fine- Jeff was getting stronger and he was using a cane and walking well. Jeff continued to improve on Saturday and Sunday until early Sunday evening when he had another seizure. It was a mild seizure, but it did paralyze his arm, and he couldn't speak but only for a few minutes. Back to Richmond we went, making phone calls to the hospital along the way. His Oncologist made arrangements for a direct admission so we wouldn't have to go to the ER and all the paperwork that goes along with it. When we arrived, we went directly to the oncology floor. Jeff's room was ready, and again the doctors were there waiting on him to get the seizure meds going into him through his IV. The next day, Jeff had a double port surgically inserted into his chest - I guess they were more certain than they let us know that Jeff's seizures were being caused by the Lymphoma. On January 13th, Jeff had brain surgery so they could biopsy the tumor. I was so scared, I was living through my worst nightmare, feeling totally helpless, and I didn't know what to do except to pray. I felt physically sick for days as we waited on the results of the biopsy. It took almost a week for the complete results, but we did know the tumor was malignant within 2 days. When Jeff's Neuro-surgeon, Dr. Tye and his Oncologist, Dr. Perkins, had the results, we learned it was definitely the Non-Hodgkin's Lymphoma. Jeff's cancer was back.

I want to go back to the day that Jeff had his biopsy. Even though Jeff was facing brain surgery, Jeff still had that sarcastic sense of humor that everyone loved. On the way to the surgical floor, Jeff was being pushed in his hospital bed by one of the transport technicians. Cris and I were walking behind them when they passed by a nurse walking in the opposite direction. Following, just a few steps behind her, was a custodian with a large broom sweeping the floor as he went along. Jeff glanced back at the transport tech and said - "Look at that - he's trying to sweep her off her feet." The tech laughed and thought it was quick thinking to come up with that comment as we passed by them. As we got to the room where Jeff would be prepped for the surgery, the nurses were talking to Jeff, and asking those routine questions. When the nurse said to Jeff – "Do you know what you're having done today?" Jeff's answer, "I'm having brain surgery...I'm going to give them a piece of my mind." That comment brought laughter to the room. The nurse told Jeff that it isn't often they get someone who is joking about going in for brain surgery. Jeff told me afterwards that when they got him to the operating room, he said to the surgeon "Could you please just take a little off the top?" Dr. Tye was glad to see that Jeff was able to be upbeat and positive and keep his sense of humor during one of the most terrifying times of his life.

As if having a brain biopsy wasn't enough, completely unexpected, Jeff woke up from the surgery totally paralyzed on his right side again. He was so upset to have lost everything he had worked so hard to gain back after he was paralyzed the first time. This time, it was very difficult for Jeff to work his way back to being able to move again. His sister, Kim, being a nurse, was able to show me how to do the range of motion exercises with him. Jeff was determined to regain movement as quickly as he could, so I did the range of motion exercises with him at least three times a day. When we weren't doing the range of motion exercises, Jeff was continually trying to raise his arm and leg on his own. Together, we made it happen – after three days, Jeff was up and trying to walk the halls. He wasn't able to go very far at first, but every day he increased the distance and eventually, he was walking laps around the oncology floor. Everyone who watched as Jeff fought to get his strength and movement back commented that they couldn't believe the determination and the effort he put forth to overcome the problems he was having. Jeff amazed many people along his journey.

The results of the biopsy were conclusive, so now Jeff's oncology team knew that they were dealing with the same demon they fought in 2006 - Non-Hodgkin's Lymphoma. Because the Lymphoma came back in his brain and central nervous system, the doctors knew, and told us, this battle would be much worse than in 2006. There were three different chemotherapy drugs that would penetrate the blood brain barrier to treat the tumor. We prayed that one of them would work for Jeff. The first one they tried was Methotrexate – one of the chemotherapy drugs they used in 2006, but in higher doses than he had in 2006. Methotrexate is a very wicked drug, especially when you are getting very high doses, so the treatments would be done as an inpatient. Jeff would have three cycles of chemo, two weeks apart. While he was in the hospital for the second cycle, Jeff had a MRI to see if there were any changes. Finally, we received some, long awaited, good news - the tumor was shrinking.

However, after the third treatment and another MRI, we heard bad news once again - the tumor was growing which meant the lymphoma had become resistant to the Methotrexate. It was time to try another chemotherapy drug, the second of three that will penetrate the blood brain barrier. The next treatment Jeff would receive was high doses of Cyterabiene which was another wicked drug. In addition to the Cyterabiene, Jeff was also going to have a lumbar puncture so a small amount of his spinal fluid would be removed and replaced with an injection of Rituxan, which are antibodies that attack cancer cells. Rituxan wasn't a new drug but injecting it into the spinal fluid was a new procedure. Jeff was the first patient at MCV to have the procedure done.

As if he didn't have enough to deal with, Jeff's right leg started to swell. We didn't think too much of it at first and thought it was probably caused by the chemo, the steroids, or a combination of both. Jeff's leg continued to swell and it got hot. However, the story changed when Jeff was admitted for chemo as this swelling was taking place, the attending physician on the oncology floor ordered a CT scan. We couldn't believe the results of the scan - Jeff had two blood clots in his lower right leg. So now, there was one more procedure Jeff had to learn to do – he had to give himself Lovenox shots (blood thinner) in his stomach.

By now it was March, and Jeff had been admitted to have his first treatment of Cyterabiene. He would also be having a lumbar puncture with the Rituxan injection each time he was admitted for a treatment. The first and second treatments were uneventful with few side effects. Jeff was admitted for his third treatment in mid-April. The second day, Jeff was half way through that treatment cycle, he woke up with a very bad headache and was nauseated. He was given pain medication which helped, and Jeff tried to stay asleep. When he woke up late in the afternoon, he wasn't feeling well at all and called the nurse for more pain medication. I was standing at Jeff's bedside when his leg began to jerk uncontrollably. I immediately called for the nurse - thank goodness there were two nurses right outside Jeff's door. Jeff was having another seizure. It was mild and didn't last long, but the look of fear in his eyes is one I will never forget. Again, Jeff had lost the use of his right side. At that point, Jeff was devastated and this was one of the only times he asked the question - WHY does this keep happening to me?"

Once again, I immediately started doing the range of motion exercises with Jeff and within two days he had regained most of his strength and movement. Jeff's oncologist stopped the chemo treatment right after the seizure and ordered another MRI. The next day, when we got the results of the MRI, we found out why he had another seizure - the tumor was growing again which meant the cancer cells had become resistant to this chemotherapy drug too. I can't begin to put into words how we felt when we had to absorb the news that the second drug had stopped working.

That afternoon, Dr. Song, the Radiation Oncologist, came to see Jeff to explain what the next course of treatment would be. Jeff would have Intense Modulated Radiation Therapy (IMRT). IMRT is used to do pinpoint radiation directly to the tumor without harming the good brain tissue. Jeff had already had his lifetime maximum of radiation because of the high doses of radiation he'd had to treat the cancer in 1992, thirteen radiation treatments to his central nervous system and brain in 2006, and the total body radiation when he had the stem cell transplant. IMRT was the only radiation option available to him. Jeff would have a total of four IMRT treatments as soon as the radiation oncology team finished the plan of treatment which would be early in May. I was concerned about waiting two weeks for the IMRT to begin and voiced that concern to Dr. Song. It was then I learned that there was a team of radiologists that would develop a very detailed, scientific plan including the exact amount of radiation and many measurements, so they could pinpoint the tumor for the radiation and not damage any good tissue in Jeff's brain. I guess I assumed it was a point, shoot, and now you're finished treatment. The radiation plan they would develop for Jeff would not take hours, but days for the team of seven to complete. When the IMRT treatments were completed, Jeff's oncologist wanted to start him on the third and final chemotherapy treatment that would penetrate the blood brain barrier. This treatment was called Temador and would start in June

Jeff finished his first round of Temador the third week of June and was feeling okay. He had an appointment with his oncologist the last week in June to get the results of the MRI that had been done after the IMRT treatments. It was a very tense drive to Richmond that day just like so many times in the past. The tense feeling turned to relief when we received the news that the IMRT was working and the tumor had begun to shrink. Since radiation continues to work long after the treatments are finished, we had every reason to believe the tumor would continue to shrink and one day it would be gone. Jeff was given the green light from Dr. Perkins to drive short distances - within two miles of his home. Jeff was so happy to be able to drive again, and I was so happy for him. Because of the seizures, he hadn't driven since January 4th when he collapsed in his office. Not being able to drive was very hard on him - he was always so independent. He took full advantage of driving too - he went someplace every day; that made me happy and I thanked God many times that Jeff was able to drive again and feel almost normal. It was wonderful to see him smiling, happy, and able to be behind the wheel of his car once again.

In July 2010, the tumor was shrinking; Jeff was driving and feeling good as his 40th birthday was approaching. Jeff was all in favor of having a birthday party to celebrate not only the BIG 40 but also that the tumor was shrinking. Since Jeff was a huge Jimmy Buffett fan, the theme for his party was one of Jeff's favorite Buffett songs – "A Pirate Looks at Forty". Pirate and tropical decorations transformed our garage into the perfect place to have the party since it was 105 degrees – in the shade - outside. We had an open house for Jeff's party from 2:00 p.m. – 10:00 p.m., so family, friends, and co-workers could stop by and spend time with Jeff on his special day. The flow of people never stopped with the last guests leaving at 10:30 p.m. It was a great day and Jeff had a wonderful time. Little did we know that the last time Jeff would be happy, smiling and having a good time would be on his 40th birthday. In the days that followed, the week after his birthday, Jeff didn't feel well and had a headache every day. Exactly one week later, on my birthday, we realized something was wrong – Jeff was having problems chewing and swallowing – it was as if his jaw didn't want to move. July 31st was the beginning of the end for my son.

Each day, the chewing problem worsened, and then Jeff began to have pain in his jaw as well as a headache. Jeff also discovered three small pea sized lumps on his body. One was on his right side, one on his left shoulder, and one on his left hip. We contacted his doctor at MCV, and Jeff went to have the lumps checked and to have blood work and scans done to see if they could determine the source of the problems he was having. The following week, Jeff had a needle biopsy done on the lump on his side which had now quadrupled in size. The headaches were coming more frequently, lasted longer, and were more painful. His doctors prescribed medications, but nothing seemed to alleviate the pain.

Our next visit was to Jeff's dentist. It seemed that because the chewing and swallowing issues continued to get worse, and he now had pain in his jaw, it could possibly have something to do with a dental problem. Along with the issues he was having with his mouth, the three tumors had grown in size and new tumors were starting to appear. The results of the needle biopsy were conclusive; there were malignant cells in the tumors. The tumor that was biopsied grew at a very rapid pace and became inflamed and eventually infected. The headaches were almost unbearable, and each day the chewing and swallowing problems were worse. The calls to the doctors were daily now along with prescriptions for pain being changed because they did little to control the pain. During all of this pain and anguish, I could see the fear in Jeff's eyes. He didn't smile much anymore, but he was still determined to keep fighting. My heart was breaking as I watched him suffer, but I was so very proud of my son for his will to live and the determination to keep fighting.

The evening of September 7th, Jeff was in so much pain, and the infection in the tumor on his side continued to get worse, and I knew we needed professional help. Cris and I took Jeff to Mary Washington Hospital in Fredericksburg, VA because by now, Jeff was in way too much pain to ride for an hour to get to his doctors at MCV in Richmond. Jeff was admitted, blood tests were done, and he had an MRI and a CT scan. The results of the tests were in – the cancer had totally invaded Jeff's body. It was then that we found out the reason Jeff was having problems with his jaw and was unable to chew anything and swallowing was extremely difficult. There was a very large tumor inside the muscle in Jeff's face that controlled the facial movements. Ironically, the original tumor in his brain that had the IMRT radiation treatments continued to shrink. Sadly, there was no possible way to radiate all the tumors that had now invaded his body. On September 9th, we were told that Jeff had only a couple weeks to live. We were living in a nightmare, and there was no longer any way out. I will never forget the sadness and fear in my son's eyes when he was told he was going to die within weeks. Jeff was devastated and unbelieving. He had just celebrated his 40th birthday and had so much he had hoped to accomplish in his next 40 years. My heart was totally broken, and I had no idea of how to deal with what was about to happen to my son. I nearly passed out when I heard the words, "Jeff will be discharged to Hospice care." How we got through everything that happened during the next three weeks is still a mystery to me. I have always believed that God won't give you more than you can handle, but hearing the word Hospice put great doubt in my mind.

The Hospice nurse and Jeff's social worker were truly wonderful and extremely patient. I knew, as Jeff's mother and having his power of attorney, I had to be the one to sign the papers for Hospice, but knowing it and being able to do it are two entirely different things. Every time I started towards the nurse's station to sign them, I started sobbing. As best as I can recall, it probably took me ten minutes to be able to approach the desk where the papers laid awaiting my signature. I picked up the pen and held it in my shaking hand still not sure I could sign those papers. The Hospice nurse, spoke to me and made me realize that not signing those papers would make it so much harder for Jeff since the Hospice nurses would be responsible for controlling Jeff's pain and keeping him as comfortable as possible. Finally, with tears dropping onto the papers, and hands that were shaking uncontrollably, I managed to put my signature on those papers. I remember dropping the pen and feeling like my heart and my world were shattered - I knew, without a miracle, I would soon lose my son and nothing would ever again be the same.

Jeff and I never gave up praying for that miracle and Jeff never once gave up his hope and determination to continue to fight. The Hospice nurse came to Jeff's room to explain everything that would be happening when he was discharged and went home. Jeff, as determined as he ever had been, looked at his nurse and said – "I hope you realize that I intend to graduate from Hospice." She smiled and told him that we would all continue to pray that he would be able to reach that goal.

At this point, Hospice took over, not only Jeff's care, but making our home comfortable for Jeff. Within hours, a hospital bed was delivered and set up, a wheel chair, a walker, and the equipment and medication for pain control were delivered. It was amazing how all these people worked together to make sure my son had everything he needed when he came home.

I could probably write three more pages about how caring, helpful, understanding, loving and supportive the Hospice care providers were. Instead, I will simply say that they were a phone call away and always there when we needed them - all hours of the day and night. I can truly say there isn't a doubt in my mind that Jeff and our family could not have made it through those two weeks Jeff was at home without the dedicated caregivers from Mary Washington Hospice.

Before Jeff was discharged from the hospital, one by one, we took care of everything that was a concern to Jeff. It was very important to him to have a will prepared. Fortunately, the husband of a very close friend, and a co-worker of Jeff's, is an attorney. He came to the hospital, computer in hand, prepared Jeff's will, found witnesses, printed a copy for Jeff's signature, and had it notarized, all within two hours.

There was something else that weighed heavily on Jeff's mind and on his heart. He needed to be sure of where he stood with God. Jeff prayed and believed in God but wasn't one who attended church every single Sunday. One of the pastors from our church came to the hospital and spoke to Jeff about his concerns. I'm not sure what was said during that conversation, but I do know that after speaking to Pastor Beth Glass, Jeff was relieved and reassured to know that as long as he believed that Jesus Christ died to save us and believed in the Divine Trinity, that God would welcome him home to have eternal life in Heaven. He realized that you don't have to be in a church to pray and believe in God.

With these two concerns taken care of, Jeff was at peace. We continued to pray for a miracle, and remained hopeful that Jeff could somehow win this battle. We could see that his condition deteriorated a little more each day. Fortunately, his pain was being controlled by medications, but Jeff could do less each day; he was often confused and slept more with each day that passed. Seeing this decline, it was obvious that the tumors in his brain were getting larger. Still, Jeff continued to tell the Hospice caregivers that he wasn't giving up hope of beating the cancer that had already taken so much from him.

Jeff was at home with us for two weeks, and we did everything we could to make his days happy, including making arrangements for Jeff to have a manicure and pedicure at home. My nail technician and wonderful friend, Kim Nguyen, made Jeff so happy that day, September 22, 2010. In fact, the last time I saw my son smile was during his pedicure. Jeff had been retaining fluid, so his legs and feet were very swollen which made him uncomfortable. As Kim was massaging his legs with cream, I said to Jeff, "Does that feel good?" He smiled and said, "It feels awesome." After the pedicure, we all sat around the dining room table to talk and have something to drink. As we were chatting, at one point I was being an over achiever in trying to help Jeff with his drink. I could tell by the way he looked at me that he wanted to do it himself. I simply said, "Ops, it's a Mom thing, but you still love me right?" Jeff started pushing his wheel chair towards me. I asked him where he was going and his reply was, "I love you so much I just want to get closer to you." What I didn't realize at the time was that those words would be the last words I would hear from my son.

Later that day, Jeff was tired and wanted to rest. He slept comfortably for a short while, but then his breathing changed, and it was clear that his pain had worsened. We called for his nurse, and within minutes she was at our home. She examined Jeff and knew things were progressing, and it was time to increase his pain medication. The increase in the medication helped for a short time, but his breathing continued to be labored. It was 3:00 a.m. – September 23, 2010 when we called his nurse again; the medication was increased again so that he would be pain free which meant Jeff would stay asleep now. Someone was with Jeff all the time – we never left his side.

His nurse told us to talk to him even though he appeared to be asleep, as there would be many times when he would be hearing us. Our family was all together and took turns sitting beside Jeff and talking to him through the night. When morning came, I knew there was no way I was leaving his room. I sat with Jeff the last twelve hours he lived, talking about many different things, holding his hand, and making promises to him about things I knew he would want to happen. Finishing his book, this book, was one of those promises.

September 23rd - our daughter - Jeff's sister, Kim, would be 43 years old. Months earlier, Jeff had purchased a special gift for Kim – a musical carousel horse that played Happy Birthday. He mentioned that gift many times during the last two weeks he was with us – it was very important to him that his sister have her gift. Although I was hesitant to leave Jeff's room, he was not alone, his father and step-mother were with him. I knew Jeff would want me to give Kim her gift on her birthday. It was about 9:30 p.m. when I went to get the gift and gave it to Kim. Tearfully, she opened the box and took out the carousel horse. I took the carousel, as Happy Birthday was playing I walked back to Jeff's room, saying, "Look Jeff, Kim has your birthday gift." As I entered his room, Happy Birthday was still playing; I laid my hand on Jeff's chest as Jeff took his last breath. I am totally certain that he heard that music box playing and knew that Kim had her birthday gift from him. We had taken care of all of his concerns except for his last gift to his sister. When that was done, Jeff felt at peace and at 9:48 p.m. on September 23, 2010, surrounded by family, Jeff went home to be with God. Jeff is finally pain free, healthy once again, and will be forever young doing God's work. One day, in God's time, we will meet again.

A hero is an ordinary individual who finds the strength to persevere and endure in spite of overwhelming obstacles.
~Christopher Reeve

Jeff is my Hero

CHAPTER 14

MOVING FORWARD...LIFE GOES ON

Throughout this book I have mentioned family and friends, suggestions they have made, and things they have done which helped me through the most difficult time in my life. I shared what they did for me and some of the suggestions they made, in this book, in hopes that everyone will realize how important family and friends can be as the journey through grief continues. I am blessed to have my family and friends help me through the grief of losing my son.

I would like to let you know how very important I feel it is to talk about your loved ones, and to keep their memory alive in your heart and in the hearts of others. I would also like to encourage everyone, who is going through the grief of losing a loved one, to keep a journal and write about your loved one and your loss. Through the promise I made to my son to finish his book, I realized that writing is great therapy. Most people probably won't want to write a book, but I hope you will write about your loved one in a journal. Write about your thoughts, your feelings, and your memories; that journal will become a treasure.

I hope reading about my journey helps you find your own path to Holding On While Letting Go. Move forward with the firm belief that you will find hope and joy again. Cherish the wonderful memories of loved ones you've lost as you strive to keep their memories alive in your heart and in the hearts of family and friends. Life will never be the same, but life will go on, you will find a new normal in your life, and it can be beautiful once again.

> *"Grief never ends…but it changes.*
> *It's a passage…not a place to stay.*
> *Grief is not a sign of weakness…nor a lack of Faith*
> *It is the price of Love."*
>
> ~Author Unknown

ABOUT THE AUTHORS

Jeff Merrifield graduated Elon College in North Carolina in 1992. He studied business administration and psychology but always had a love of journalism.

Cancer would change Merrifield's career path. Employed by Prince William County Schools in Northern Virginia, he worked in administration as a security officer, mentoring many students during his seventeen years of employment. Jeff touched the lives of many people and his legacy lives on in many ways.

Sharon Crislip, Jeff's mother, is retired from Prince William County schools, and now has her own business under the logo of Coastal Creations. She and her husband enjoy traveling around the country in their RV, something Jeff wanted them to do. Sharon promised her son, on the day he died, she would finish the book he started, and would have *Holding on While Letting Go* published. She is now able to fulfill that promise.

Made in the USA
Middletown, DE
20 September 2015